Can I Tell You About...

Auditory Processing Disorder?

CAN I TELL YOU ABOUT...?

The 'Can I tell you about...?' series offers simple introductions to a range of conditions, issues and big ideas that affect our lives. Friendly characters invite readers to learn about their experiences, share their knowledge, and teach us to empathise with others. These books serve as excellent starting points for family and classroom discussions.

Other subjects covered in the Can I tell you about...? series

ADHD	Gender Diversity
Adoption	Gratitude
Anxiety	Loneliness
Asperger Syndrome	ME/Chronic Fatigue
Asthma	Syndrome
Autism	Multiple Sclerosis
Bipolar Disorder	OCD
Cerebral Palsy	Parkinson's Disease
Compassion	Pathological Demand
Dementia	Avoidance Syndrome
Depression	Peanut Allergy
Diabetes (Type 1)	Selective Mutism
Down Syndrome	Self-Harm
Dyslexia	Sensory Processing
Dyspraxia	Difficulties
Eating Disorders	Stammering/Stuttering
Eczema	Stroke
Epilepsy	Tourette Syndrome

Can I Tell You About...

Auditory Processing Disorder?

A Guide for Friends, Family and Professionals

Alyson Mountjoy

Illustrated by Kelly Davies

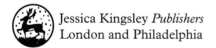
Jessica Kingsley *Publishers*
London and Philadelphia

First published in 2018
by Jessica Kingsley Publishers
73 Collier Street
London N1 9BE, UK
and
400 Market Street, Suite 400
Philadelphia, PA 19106, USA

www.jkp.com

Library of Congress Cataloging in Publication Data
A CIP catalog record for this book is available
from the Library of Congress

British Library Cataloguing in Publication Data
A CIP catalogue record for this book is
available from the British Library

ISBN 978 1 78592 494 1
eISBN 978 1 78450 883 8

Printed and bound in Great Britain

MIX
Paper from
responsible sources
FSC® C013056

CONTENTS

DEDICATION AND ACKNOWLEDGEMENTS

I dedicate this book to my son, the reason that I started on this Auditory Processing Disorder (APD) journey so many years ago. I honour his individuality, kindness and empathy, and all the gifts that make him special, just like every other child with APD. Because of him, I co-founded the first UK voluntary group for APD with other like-minded parents. It led to the online groups, documents, articles, newsletters and support that I have provided for almost 18 years, all of which has led me here.

The book is also dedicated to my friends and online group members worldwide who have shared my journey. They are the parents and adults with APD who support each other through the darkest of days, despite their own struggles. They have taught me so much, and I thank them. I also dedicate this book to the supportive professionals and researchers who work tirelessly to further APD diagnosis and recognition in the UK and beyond. Alongside them, parents are fighting for UK-wide specialist APD testing centres to the standard set by the few already established. We need many more, and soon.

Last, but by no means least, I thank the rest of my family and friends for their continued support, particularly Kelly Davies, the talented illustrator who brought this book to life.

In this book, I aim to help children with APD to understand their condition. I want them to know that with determination and the right support, they can make their dreams come true. But it is also to help parents to understand APD, access accurate diagnosis and full support for their children at school and at home, or when home educating. It is also for teachers and other professionals, to help them understand how APD affects children in real-life terms and how to best support them all in the way that they need – APD support must be tailored. Also, children with APD need acceptance, patience, time and understanding. Every child has a right to the best education and a positive future. We must get it right first time, every time.

INTRODUCTION FOR ADULTS

Auditory Processing Disorder is a condition that affects the way that the brain processes sound, including speech. In people with APD, their brain doesn't properly understand what they hear, although their hearing itself is not normally affected. Please remember, with APD:

- effects can change from day to day, and even within a day

- effects are worse when the person is ill, stressed or tired

- the pattern of difficulties is unique to each individual

- slight improvement might occur as a child gets older, but APD is for life

- it qualifies as a disability, sometimes causing safety issues (e.g. traffic, fire alarms)

- all areas of life are affected, via difficulties with communicaton and understanding speech

- self-esteem, confidence, social skills and relationships are often affected

- children with APD can be isolated and vulnerable, even bullied

- stress and anxiety are common, especially without full support

- intelligence is not affected.

There will normally be other unrelated conditions or difficulties that can make APD harder to cope with (and vice versa). Children with suspected APD must be referred for specialist testing for APD and other co-existing difficulties. First, they need to be tested by a speech and language therapist and an educational psychologist, to confirm or rule out any other conditions before referral for APD testing. Only a specialist in audiology/audio-vestibular medicine is qualified to diagnose APD. Please check the testing criteria for the testing centre you choose, and that full APD testing is given.

Children with APD should:

- be encouraged to develop coping strategies – ways to get around the APD and other difficulties

- receive help in learning how APD affects them, and how to describe its effects

- be encouraged and supported to learn self-advocacy skills – how to describe and request the help they need, both as children and later as adults

- receive full school support for APD and all other difficulties, tailored in the way that they need it, plus provision of any recommended equipment

- use their preferred learning style, compensatory gifts and skills to help them, at school and throughout life.

The only way to secure appropriate, legally guaranteed support for a child with education, health and care needs is for parents and guardians to apply to the local authority for an education, health and care plan/EHCP (England) or a statement of educational needs (Wales, Scotland and N.I.). It should include support for their APD, all other diagnosed conditions, and physical and mental health problems. It should also include equipment, for example the purchase, maintenance and insurance of an FM system (a wireless assistive hearing device), if recommended on testing. Without such a plan or statement, your school might not be able to give your child all the help they need, deserve and are entitled to receive in order to access an appropriate education.

In this way, success is possible for *any* child with APD, to the best of their own ability, whatever level that might be.

Here are some common APD difficulties. Although people might have a different mixture of them, you don't have to have all of them. APD means that you might not be able to:

- understand sounds and words, even familiar ones

- perceive gaps between sounds and words

- remember what people say to you, or ask you to do

- remember what is said or asked in the right order

- know the direction of someone who is speaking, or who to listen to (if there is more than one person talking or you are in a group)

- process the sound of alarm clocks, bells or fire alarms

- estimate how close you are to moving cars when crossing the road (by sound)

- understand and decipher speech when it's noisy – words get mixed up with the noise

- process, understand or remember what is said for a long time after (delayed processing)

- process or remember the start, middle or end of a sentence (or any of it).

APD can lead to other difficulties too in:

- using the phone

- understanding people with strong accents

- holding what is said in your head long enough to do something with it

- getting used to new people and their voice patterns – you might understand male voices better, or find it easier processing female voices

- speech, reading or spelling – from not processing or using speech sounds properly, or forgetting them.

APD can sometimes be confused with other conditions. Some symptoms seem similar, but they have a different cause. It is more difficult to work out what's wrong when a child with APD has other conditions too. These children have complex difficulties; that's why full, multi-discipline testing is important. They will also need full, tailored support – at home, at school and later as adults with APD in adult education and at work. APD is for life.

"I'm Amy and I have Auditory Processing Disorder, or APD. You may not think it to look at me because APD is invisible. That means that the signs are hidden. Although many thousands of children might have APD, it isn't well known.

APD is a medical condition. My brain doesn't understand sound and speech properly. APD makes it hard to understand what people say to me. It's worse in noisy places, because words get lost in the noise.

My hearing is fine, I just can't always understand what I hear. My brain makes mistakes, not my ears. People with hearing loss can have APD too. APD isn't a learning difficulty itself, but it can cause them in some people.

APD has different causes too. Some children are born with it. But the cause doesn't really matter. It's the way it affects us that is important.

Everyone has different symptoms and effects of APD. People with APD normally have other conditions and difficulties too. They can make it harder to cope with the APD. You need testing for all of them, so that you can get the right help.

I struggle at school in lots of ways because of APD. The way APD affects me can change a lot through the day. The effects can come and go. Sometimes I can understand everything, but at other times all the words get jumbled up. Then I can only understand a few words. When my APD is very bad, nothing makes sense. It can be worse when I'm ill, tired or worried about things, which can happen a lot. I sometimes get left behind while people are talking around me. My friend Tom has APD too, but his APD is different.

Because APD isn't always the same, some people think that I'm making it up. It makes me sad when people don't understand. Sometimes I get annoyed with myself when I can't follow what people say. It's important that anyone who might have APD is tested. This helps them understand that it isn't their fault.

APD has no cure. It can improve a little on its own up to the age of 12 or 13, but it never goes away. I will always have APD. So, it is up to me to understand how it affects me, and work out ways to live with it and get around it. I have to learn to explain it to other people too. If I can do that, they will know the right sort of help to give me. Then I can get a good job when I leave school. Let me explain..."

"When I was little, Mum noticed that I seemed not to hear or understand what was said to me. She took me for a hearing test, but it was normal. My hearing was fine, and it made no sense. It was worse when I was out playing or in a group. I struggled to understand if it was noisy, if music was playing, or the TV was on. I had problems remembering what was said to me too, sometimes for a long time afterwards. I couldn't remember what Mum and Dad asked me to do. Sometimes I remembered things in the wrong order. This happened most of the time. I used to get upset. Now I know that these were signs of APD.

One day, someone told Mum about APD and she joined an online group. Other parents told her that children like me have a medical problem with our brain, and I needed to be tested. Testing is the only way to know if you have APD. You must find out how it affects you.

Mum found out I needed to see someone called a specialist audiologist. They have proper training. They know what tests to use, and they can understand the results. Nobody else can do it. First, I had to have reports to show how I was doing in school, and to look for any other difficulties. So, I had testing done at school. These tests don't diagnose APD, but sometimes they give signs that you need testing. The tests also showed that I have trouble with numbers. My friend Tom had tests too; he has other difficulties. None of these problems are caused by the APD, but they make school harder for us."

"There are rules about who can be tested for APD. Your parents need to check because each testing centre is different. Tom had glue ear when he was little, and it caused hearing loss that came and went. So, he couldn't have APD tests until the glue ear had gone and his hearing was normal again. That was when they found out Tom was sensitive to sound. If you have hearing loss, you need extra tests that take longer. Some clinics can't do it. They don't test children who have certain other conditions, or children who have problems with speech and answering questions. They need to know the results are because of APD, and caused by just APD (not by hearing loss or anything else).

Our local doctor sent me for another hearing test. That was normal too. So, Mum asked her to send a letter (called a referral) to the APD testing centre. Normally you have to be at least 7 to be tested. The doctor sent the referral along with all my other reports. Then I had to wait a few months for an appointment.

Mum explained that the APD tests were nothing to worry about, and she was right. On the day, Mum came with me to the APD clinic. First, we had a talk with the specialist. Mum explained my difficulties at home and at school. They talked about my reports and a form that they sent my school to fill in. Then I was taken to sit in a quiet room. I had to listen through headphones to different sounds and words, and answer some questions about what I heard. That was the testing. Mum or Dad could have come in with me if I wanted, but I was OK by myself.

The tests took a couple of hours. I was tired by the end, but you can ask for a break if you need one. After the tests, the specialist explained the results to Mum. You have to have two or more difficulties of a certain level for a full diagnosis of APD. If you have one, or more than one but they aren't very bad, they say you have auditory processing difficulties. Children with that diagnosis still need help at school too. We were sent a report a few weeks later with the results, and ways that my school should help me. The report said that I had a full diagnosis of APD."

"Children with APD have good days and bad days. On a good day, I can understand more. But even on good days I might not understand everything. APD can be worse at different times of the day too. When I'm ill, tired or upset, it's more difficult to understand and remember anything I'm told. I need people to be patient with me.

Mum read in her online support group that she should always get my attention and look at me when she spoke to me. She found out that I needed to read her lips and see her face to help me understand what she meant. I didn't even know I was doing it. You might find that you already do this too.

After my diagnosis, Mum helped me to understand how APD affected me. It made me really happy to know that not understanding people wasn't my fault. I wasn't just stupid or lazy, like some children said. Mum also found out that APD could run in families, but that doesn't mean that everyone in the family will have it. My sister Lucy doesn't have APD. Dad had always had problems understanding people, although his difficulties were different

to mine. He thought he might have APD too.
They can also test adults. My friend Tom and
Dad have been tested now, and they both have
a diagnosis of APD as well.

Everyone copes in different ways, and it
helps to find ways around APD. Before my
diagnosis, nobody understood why sometimes
I could understand them and other times I
couldn't. Only Mum and Dad would believe
me. Lucy understands now, and we get on
much better. Children with APD need people to
believe them."

"Children with APD get very tired from trying to understand what they hear. After school, we need a quiet place to rest our brain, relax and process what we heard during the day. We need to be left alone to do that. It's very important that our families understand, and we get this quiet time. Our brains are like sponges and we can only soak up so much sound in a day. By the time I get home from school, nothing more will go in. It's all just noise.

Kids with APD can get upset, worried or sad. Sometimes our teachers (and even our parents) don't understand how tired we are, how hard we try, or how much we hate to fail all the time. It can make us upset or angry because our day at school was so bad. I try to hold it all in until I get home, in case I get told off by my teacher. It can be very upsetting. Since my diagnosis, other people in my family are starting to understand about APD too, and that helps me a lot. But some people still won't believe there's anything wrong with me, and that can be very hurtful.

I can't tell Mum about what happened at school until hours after I get home, or maybe the next day. I just don't remember. Although Tom forgets a lot of what he hears because of his APD, he remembers everything he sees. Mum told me it helps him cope with APD. Sometimes, at bedtime, it all goes around in his head like a video and keeps him awake. It helps to tell his mum about his day, then he can sleep. Other children with APD can have problems sleeping too. That makes them more tired the next day, then coping with APD is even harder. It's worse when they're worried or upset about school, people don't understand them or they have no help. It helps to tell your mum or dad."

"People who don't know about APD can't see why we don't understand them or get things wrong. They may think we're stupid, but we're not. We can find it hard to put together an answer. They can get fed up of waiting, or they change the subject. We might not understand when someone is joking, or we get upset for no reason because we think children are being hurtful. But sometimes they are.

A few children stopped speaking to me and Tom. They gave up trying to be friends with us. Some children with APD choose to stop trying to make friends, because it's so difficult. They get fed up of getting things wrong and being upset. It can be easier not to bother; but it can get lonely. It helps to know that I'm not the only person with APD, and that I can't help it.

Children with APD can get upset and angry at school too, like Tom. Sometimes it all gets too much. Some children tease and bully children with APD and other difficulties. If that happens to you, or if you get upset or need help, you must tell an adult like your mum, dad or a teacher.

I met Tom when I started school. It was really noisy, so he used to put his hands over

his ears. Mum saw that Tom had signs of
APD like me. So, she told his mum. Then she
understood that Tom needed to be tested too.
Many children with APD find it hard to make
and keep friends. I'm lucky that I have a good
friend like Tom. He understands about APD,
even if his APD is different from mine.

If your friends always meet up in a group
or in noisy places, it can be very hard to
understand them. It helps to talk where it's
quiet. It's worse if people all speak at the same
time. If the person with APD misses part of
what someone says or gets the meaning wrong,
it can lead to arguments."

"People with APD have to learn about how their APD affects them so that they can understand it. But it's just as important to learn to talk to other people about it. You need to find your own way to tell people what it means to have APD, and how they can help you. They won't know if you don't tell them.

Mum and Dad asked me to tell them how APD makes things difficult for me. Sometimes I can't say the words, so I write it down and show them. You can try that too. Parents can help by telling people for us, but they are not always with us, especially at school.

Teachers can help too when they understand about APD and know what you need. Last week, Mum came into school and helped me to give a talk to my class about my APD. You can do that if you like, once you learn about it and understand what you need people to do

to help you. You can say it in different ways.
I always start with: 'I have Auditory Processing
Disorder, or APD.' I explain that there's
nothing wrong with my hearing, then I add
something else, like this, to show how it affects
me: 'It's like my brain has faulty wiring,' or,
'Sometimes, what I hear doesn't make sense.'

It can help to practise at home, trying
different ways to say it. I always carry an APD
alert card to show to people, and so does Tom.
Even Dad has one. It explains about APD,
and it has some helpful tips. Your parents can
carry one to show people. You can carry one
too. It helps if you can't find the right words
to describe APD, or what you need people to
do. You can show it to your teachers or other
children. You should never be afraid to ask for
help when you need it, for your APD or your
other difficulties.

It helps me if people get my attention before speaking to me, by saying my name. Then I can look at them and read their lips. I also ask people to speak clearly and not too quickly. They need to use simple words and short sentences, and ask me to do one thing at a time. Some people, like me, may need to have things repeated word for word; others need it worded in a different way, or written down. Other people, like Tom, find it easier to look at pictures or drawings. You may need to ask for something else. Only you will know what you need.

It isn't easy learning about APD, or telling people what you need. It takes time and practice. But it can help you a lot once you learn how to do it. Now I understand more about APD and my other difficulties. So, I'm better at it than I used to be. If I can do it, you can too."

"When I started school, I used to get into trouble for not listening. My teachers told my parents that I needed to pay attention and work harder. But I knew I was trying my best. Even if children with APD try hard and listen in class, it still doesn't make sense. It's really tiring, and everything takes us a lot longer. Often, we don't finish our work. It takes longer when we don't understand what the teacher asks us to do. I used to get told off for asking too many questions, or asking other children. I just needed help. Tom used to get into trouble for arguing with the teachers. They said something different from what he thought they said. But he wasn't trying to cause trouble. It can be very confusing when you can't believe what you hear.

After my diagnosis, Mum took my report to school. At first, my school didn't know anything about APD. Some schools don't believe APD exists, even if a child has a specialist diagnosis. But I was lucky. Mum took in lots of information and my teachers learned all about APD and how it affects me. They agreed to do what the specialist recommended. Every child with APD needs different support, for the APD and all the other conditions that they might have.

My report said that the classroom should be made quieter, using things like rugs and posters. I needed an FM system to help me to understand the teacher when it's noisy. Now I have one, and so does Tom. We can't follow lessons properly without it. The teacher wears a microphone and we wear headsets. But some people prefer to wear earpieces called ear moulds, made to fit inside their ears. Not all children with APD need an FM system, but they must be able to try one if they need one."

"There are some ways to help all children with APD at school, as well as providing what they need on an individual basis. It's very important to be given all our class notes, already typed for us. When Tom and I make notes, they have parts missing because of our APD. Also, what we write down is often wrong. Before diagnosis, our tests and exam results were always bad. That's because we had to learn from the notes we made. Now, Tom and I get the typed notes a few days before the lesson is taught in class, with a list of new words. Because we have trouble remembering what we hear in the right order, we have instructions written down too. Lessons make more sense, and our test marks are much better now.

Sometimes our brains just switch off when there's too much noise or information. It isn't because we aren't trying. So, it helps that we can ask for extra breaks in a quiet place when listening gets too much. Now we take all our tests and exams in a quiet room, and we get extra time to let us process things. All children with APD need this support.

We can also have trouble remembering the right words to use when writing answers, and problems holding numbers in our head to do sums. Timed tests are very difficult. It's worse when the questions are spoken, so we don't have those sorts of tests now. We also have homework that has been altered to take less time, so we get less tired.

You may not need all these things, and you might need different help as well. I also need help with maths, and Tom wears ear defenders to block sound when he needs to. He's sensitive to other things too, and this takes his attention away from what he should be doing. Tom and I are much happier now; we don't have to worry about school and Tom has stopped getting into trouble. We still get things wrong, but not as much, and we know it isn't our fault. Now we have a chance to do our best, like other children.

There may be several children with APD at every school. I wish our school had known about APD before we were diagnosed. They could have helped us sooner, and we wouldn't have had to struggle so much to learn. Because the teachers already knew about my APD when Tom was tested, it was easier for him to get help.

People with APD can be just as clever as anyone else. They can do well at school and get a good job, if they get the right sort of help all the time. You can use your hobbies and interests, and what you're best at. Not all children are good at exams, even with help. But they might be good at things like art, sports, music or making things. My teacher says I'm good at writing stories. I want to go to college and be a writer. Tom is good at football and other sports. He wants to be a footballer or a sports teacher. With the right sort of help, I know we will succeed.

Work hard, believe in yourself, and you can make your dreams come true too."

HOW TO HELP

Every child with APD needs family, friends and teachers to learn about it, and know how to help them. If you know someone with APD, here are some ways that you can help:

- Talk to them somewhere quiet, avoid places with background noise that blocks speech, and turn off the TV or music.

- Look at them when you speak – use their name.

- Speak clearly – use short sentences and plain words.

- Be patient – give them time to process what you say, and extra time to answer.

- Encourage them to carry an APD alert card, help them to explain about APD and ways to help.

- Let them tell you what helps them – they may need something repeated or said in a different way, or some other help.

- If they don't tell you how to help, ask what you can do.

- Take turns talking in a group; lots of voices can be harder to understand.

- Using the phone can be difficult for people with APD – text or email instead.

- Online voice chat with friends can be difficult with APD – use online text chat instead.

- People with APD get very tired and need to rest. It doesn't mean they don't want friends or dislike having fun. Don't leave them out.

- If your friend with APD is being picked on or bullied, tell an adult.

Remember: a person with APD is not stupid or lazy, or different from you; they just need a little help to understand what they hear. Always be patient and kind. Let them know that they aren't alone.

Reading this book will already be helping you to understand APD. Ask your family, friends, teachers and other adults to read it too. Tell others about APD and how to help. Then all children with APD will get the best chance to be whatever they choose.

INFORMATION AND SUPPORT

APD Support UK is a voluntary organisation formed in 2017, seeking wider recognition, standardised testing and full support for APD, both in the UK and internationally.

The APD Support UK website – https://apdsupportuk.yolasite.com – has information and articles based on many years of research and experience. It also has links to Facebook groups with support and advice on diagnosis, education and work support for families and those with APD and co-existing conditions. Supportive professionals are welcome.

DEPUTY D/
Or
D. B. COOPER,

a Mary MacIntosh novel

Debi,
Enjoy true
Crime.

Maureen

MAUREEN ANNE MEEHAN

DEPUTY DAWG
Or
D. B. COOPER,

Copyright © 2024 by Maureen Anne Meehan

ISBN: 979-8-3304-3439-8 (e)

www. maureenmeehanbooks.com

info@maureenmeehan.com

Author's Note

She was knocked down far many times

For every step she took, she had to put up a fight

Having the courage to choose was her only way

With every hope that came her way, dark was there to dim the light…

Friends turned her down

A young dreamer from a small town.

It was all so new

The days were different from the morning dew

She had to face the wrath she didn't know why

Everyone she met had something to lie

How she sat alone

Vulnerable to life and prone

Wondering where her guardian Angels were

The future seemed to blur…

Losing the idea of life, she decided to hold on to survive every single day

The only savior she had was her dream

In a place full of people where success is what they scream…

Now, she looks back and smiles

To all the people who unintentionally made her strong

Rising to the top after crawling the miles

She learned that a good heart overcomes the wrong

This Author's Note is borrowed, in part, from an anonymous poem. It has been modified to meet the author's needs, but it is not a truly original thought.

Table of Contents

Dedication

Deputy Dawg or D. B. Cooper, is dedicated to all true-crime enthusiasts. You know who you are. You love an unsolved crime more than a solved one, as the mystery remains alive.

The portion of the novel deals with the murder of Sheriff Guy Howard Gaughnor in Nederland, Colorado, in 1971. May this hero rest in peace.

The portion of the novel concerning D. B. Cooper's hijacking is dedicated to flight attendant Florence Schaffner, who kept her wits about her during the hijacking of Northwest Orient Airline flight 305 from Portland to Seattle on November 24, 1971. There are crew and passengers who likely owe their lives to this woman.

This novel is also dedicated to a few people who helped educate me on these crimes. One is to a man I met at a bar on Pearl Street in Boulder while waiting for my daughter to finish a photo shoot and return to our cabin outside of Nederland, Colorado. He told me about Deputy Dawg. I never got his name. In addition, Ferrell Ostrow told me about D. B. Cooper. I was unaware of this hijacking, likely as a result of growing up in the small town of Sheridan, Wyoming. Not many people with whom I was raised were aware of it, but it appears that everyone else in the United States was and is.

When creating this combination of true crime and fiction, I became patently aware that these two crimes happened within a few months of each other in 1971 and how fun it could be to unite them in Wyoming with Mac.

The cover is dedicated to Dalen Lawrence who is a mastermind creator in both business and AI. He understood what I was looking for in a cover and instantaneously created it and sent it to me. Brilliant.

And as always, I dedicate this to my family, friends, and readers. I could not do this without your support and encouragement.

Chapter 1

Renner Forbes was the beloved Sheriff in Nederland, Colorado in 1971. On July 17, 1971, Sheriff Forbes was sitting at The Pioneer Inn having an aft-shift drink when Guy Gaughnor entered the bar. Forbes was a former Air Force pilot who served in World War II, Vietnam, and Korea it was said that he had a distaste for "hippies" especially the STP Family "cult" of hippie drug dealers similar to the Charles Manson-type.

STP was the "Serenity, Tranquility and Peace" cult from New York, and they were quite akin to the Manson west coast of hippie druggie criminals who terrorized the towns they occupied.

STP was run out of New York for drug crime in the late sixties, and they made their way west landing in what was known to be liberal Boulder, Colorado. The STP Family were identified as the dirtiest, smelliest people of the entire early 1970s freak scene and they found their new digs near the "Beach" of Boulder Creek near the University of Colorado, Boulder campus at the base of the Flatiron mountains.

These filthy hippies occupied a house near frat row, and one could take off a jar of honey spiked with acid on their front porch.

They all had monikers or nicknames like Skrat, and they were always tripping on illicit drugs, and they loved to "konk" college kids walking to class by throwing stuff at them. They were sallow-skinned with poor grooming and gleeful expressions of Vietnam Vets high on drugs and a penchant for guns.

STPs drank a lot, including Cisco, 20/20, Strawberry Hill, Annie Green Springs, Schlitz, Miller, and their favorite, Kool-Aid Ever clear, which they called Purple Jesus. They hosted loud, cantankerous parties, and needless to say, the alcohol, drugs, and guns sometimes did not blend.

Nicknames were a penchant, and one could find STP hippies named Deputy Dawg, Grody, Patty Rotten Crotch, LB Rabbit, Candy, Charles B. Beard, Daisy May, Asshole Dave, and Mike Motherfucker. These pleasant people peddled a drug called Owsley, which was a variant of MDA and kept people tripping for days.

They peddled a drug called Owsley, which was a variant of MDA that kept people tripping for days. This drug was what caused law enforcement to drive them out of the lower east side of New York City, and they migrated to what was known as the freak haven of Boulder, Colorado.

STP hippies were a filthy lot, reeking of body odor, cigarettes, booze, pot, and urine.

They wore tattered, dirty clothing that had the overall appearance of something that had been worn for years, rolled in the dirt, stained with urine and feces, and possibly dropped down a coal mine shaft. It was a sight.

One STP gal used to beg for money outside Canyon Liquors wearing a child's baby doll dress as a shirt and greasy leather biker's pants that were about six inches too long which she slit in the front to make room for her toes, and the remainder of the leather leggings dragged behind her when she walked.

The best STP accessories were obtainable in the mountains, such as animal furs, which were skinned and sewn on as patches for torn clothing, and bleached animal skulls that were worn as hats.

They would trip out on drugs and hoot and holler, and one STP guy used to roll in the mud yelling, "Fuck the lucky ducky" over and over.

One time there was a day festival at Hidden Valley Ranch when one of the STPs named Russ wore a cape made of leaves, twigs, burrs, mud, bugs and excrement. It was quite the visual. His face was bleeding, and he was so wasted that he fell into the bonfire, and his cape went up in flames.

One STP gal used to walk through the park topless, and she answered to her nickname, Lady Jane. She would wear a pristine white Victorian dress made of ripped lace, revealing her breasts, and she did not seem to have a care in the world.

Other ladies from the STP cult had nicknames such as Patty Rotten Crotch and the Skank Sisters, who were often found wandering around with Lady Jane chanting "spare change for dog food" for no apparent reason.

Charlie Blackbeard wore an old union suit with a homemade T-shirt that he had written STP on it. Once, he was playing pool at a local bar with a pal named Eddie Spaghetti, and every time Charlie Blackbeard bent over the table to take a shot, one could see his crusty butt crack.

Embroidery was all the rage in 1971, with hippies in general. Popular apparel items included Gram Parson's Nudie suits and chunky heels with tight, high-waisted jackets.

Hippie stores sold Ed Roth hot-rod T-shirts that said, "Wrap Your Ass in Fiberglass." Plastic t-strap Mary Jane shoes in lime green were popular, and t-shirts with cartoon characters like Rooty Toot Toot and Rupert Bear were all the rage.

Nederland, Colorado, is a charming mountain town located in Boulder County, about 16 miles west of Boulder. Situated at an elevation of around 8,230 feet, it's known for its scenic beauty, outdoor recreation, and vibrant community. Nederland serves as a gateway to the nearby Indian Peaks Wilderness and Roosevelt National Forest, making it a popular spot for hiking, mountain biking, and winter sports like skiing and snowshoeing.

The town has a unique, laid-back vibe with a mix of artists, musicians, and outdoor enthusiasts. It hosts several popular events, including Frozen Dead Guy Days, a quirky winter festival that celebrates an unusual local story about a cryogenically frozen man. Nederland also has a small but lively downtown area with local shops, cafes, and live music, reflecting its eclectic and creative spirit.

Nederland always had a hippie feel to it, and the most popular bar was the Pioneer Inn, which was on the main drag. They served 3.2 beer back in 1971, and it was the Pioneer Inn where the Sheriff got into it with STP Guy Gaughnor. Gaughnor was a town nuisance, and he was known to pop off to the Sheriff when he was at the Pioneer.

He went by the moniker "Deputy Dawg," who was a cartoon character as part of the Terry town series entitled "Deputy Dawg," which aired in the late '60s and early 70's, featuring a bumbling but well-intentioned sheriff who tries to enforce the law in a Southern town, often getting into humorous situations.

One evening in 1971, Forbes was in an especially cantankerous mood, and the Sheriff was not impressed. After the Sheriff finished his beer and headed home for the night, Gaughnor uttered his one last slur, which was the final straw for the Sheriff.

Sheriff Forbes ushered Deputy Dawg out of the Pioneer Inn and told him to get lost. Deputy Dawg did not like how the Sheriff was treating him, and he made his feelings known to the patrons. This last uttering caught the attention of all in attendance.

Chapter 2

Sheriff Forbes was a no-nonsense officer of the law, and he was not going to tolerate the STP hippies and their drug-induced cult like behaviors.

He especially disliked Guy "Deputy Dawg" Gaughnor, who was young, stupid, and sassy with a penchant for popping off while intoxicated. He was openly defiant, argumentative, and intentionally antagonistic.

He had been arrested multiple times in both Boulder and Nederland, and Sheriff Forbes usually took him for booking in Boulder if he arrested him in Nederland because Forbes did not want him in his jail in Nederland.

On this particular evening of July 17, 1971, Forbes was sick of this abusive, antagonistic, hostile hippie. Forbes had a military mindset and was direct and confrontational with Gaughnor. He put Gaughnor in his gold 1868 Plymouth and drove away. It was the last time anyone in Nederland ever saw Forbes.

It wasn't long before the Sheriff was reported missing, and an APB was put out regarding Guy Gaughnor. He was the only suspect in the case of the missing person. It was no secret in town that there was no love lost between the two men.

About a month later, hunters discovered the Sheriff's skull near an abandoned gold mine just off Oh My God Road, which is about 25 miles northeast of Nederland in Clear Creek County.

It was easy to identify the skull as the Sheriff had a distinctive look with one missing tooth and two teeth that overlapped one another.

Deputy Dawg was on the lam. He was not seen for decades.

Chapter 3

On November 24, 1971, a mere three months after Deputy Dawg disappeared from Nederland, Colorado, a man hijacked Northwest Orient Airlines flight 305 from Portland, Oregon, to Seattle, Washington D. B. Cooper, also known as Dan Cooper, was one of the last passengers to purchase a one-way ticket to board the Boeing 727 aircraft and he sat in the back row purposefully near where the flight attendants prepared drinks.

He was a white male with dark hair and brown eyes wearing a black business suit with a white shirt and a thin black necktie.

He ordered a bourbon and 7-Up from the flight attendant, and when she served it to him, he gave her a note she mistakenly thought it was a pickup line as it was common in this era for flight attendants to be very attractive females and they were hit on willy nilly by men. She slipped the unread note in her purse and carried on.

He pulled her aside and said, "Miss, you had better read that note. I have a bomb."

This alarmed her a bit as he was in a business suit wearing sunglasses and she immediately got that tingly feeling in her stomach. She returned to her purse and fetched his note and read it.

In neat all capital letters with a felt-tip pen she read the print that stated, "Miss – I have a bomb in my briefcase and want you to sit by me."

She returned the note to hijacker D. B. Cooper, sat down as requested, and asked him if she could see the bomb.

She did not believe him at first and so he opened his briefcase to reveal four sticks of what she believed to be dynamite hooked together by wires and some sort of device. Now her heart was jumping, and she did not know what to do. He demanded $200,000 in ramson, which would be the equivalent of $1,500,000 in 2024, and requested four very specific types of parachutes upon landing in Seattle.

The flight attendant informed the captain that there was a problem on board, and the crew radioed Seattle-Tacoma International Airport about this emergency situation and informed them of the hijacker's demands.

The captain informed everyone on board that there was an issue without being specific and told them that they would need to circle Sea-Tac until instructed to land. The mission was to allow emergency response personnel to gather the demands, including the money and specific parachutes, and to allow ground forces to prepare for what could lie ahead.

They circled Seattle for about two hours while arrangements were being made on the ground.

It was raining hard on this day before Thanksgiving, so it did not surprise the passengers that they might be circling in hopes of the weather clearing.

The reality was that they were circling in order for the money to be gathered in the specific manner requested and that these rare parachutes could be summoned from a local air base and a sky diving company.

The flight attendant continued to sit next to the hijacker, and she started chatting with him. At first, she started by identifying cities below them as they circled, and then she graduated to conversations more pertinent to the issue at hand. She asked him why he chose Northwest Airlines to hijack. His response was, "It's not because I have a grudge against your airlines; it's just because I have a grudge," then, explained that this flight simply suited his needs. He asked where she was from, and she replied that she was originally from Pennsylvania but was living in Minnesota at the time. She asked where he was from, and he became upset and refused to answer. If asked if she smoked and offered her a cigarette, she replied that she had quit, but she accepted the cigarette.

Another passenger stopped to chat on his way to use the restroom, and he inquired about the reason for the delay with the flight attendant D. B. Cooper initially appeared amused by the interaction but quickly became annoyed with the conversation and told the man in the cowboy hat to take his seat and leave them alone.

However, the cowboy ignored Cooper and continued his conversation with the flight attendant; however, Cooper's increased annoyance made the cowboy return to his seat.

He said to the flight attendant, "If that is a sky marshal, I don't want any more of that," but she reassured him that there were no sky marshals on that flight.

The $200,000 ransom was received from Seattle First National Bank in a bag weighing nearly 20 pounds, and by 5:46 p.m. on November 24, 1971, Flight 305 landed at Sea-Tac.

Once the demands had been sequestered on the tarmac of Sea-Tac, the plane was allowed to land. The captain followed air traffic control instructions to park the aircraft a long way away from the terminal so that if the bomb was detonated, it would not harm folks on the ground. Cooper agreed that the captain could park the airplane on a partially lit runway, away from the main terminal.

Cooper demanded that only one representative of the airline approach the aircraft's front door using a mobile stairway.

With the passengers remaining seated, the airline representative approached the airplane with the ransom money and parachutes. Cooper then agreed to release the passengers. The passengers deplaned. They were safely bussed to the terminal, and it was only then that they learned of the true facts on board.

The media met these passengers in the terminal, and when interviewed, the passengers were in utter shock to learn that they were aboard a hijacked aircraft.

The hijacker then instructed the ground crew to refuel the aircraft. He had kept all six of the crew members on board. He told the captain via the flight attendant that he had passed the note that he had a flight plan that needed to be filed as they were going to refuel in Seattle and take off to Mexico City with a stop in Reno to refuel once again. This was communicated with aircraft control and the flight plan was initiated.

Within 30 minutes of takeoff from Sea-Tac, he instructed the captain to fly the Boeing 727 at an altitude of 10,000 feet, which was highly unusual, but the captain obliged after confirming with air traffic control and kept the aircraft right at 10,000 feet.

The hijacker had obliviously premeditated this event as he then instructed the captain of the pitch of the flaps and that the wheels had to remain down during the flight.

Chapter 4

Chaos interrupted in Nederland. Despite the 70s, there were still some sane folks who were simply mountain people, and the STP cult was simply that. A cult. Menacing hippies.

Charles Manson's followers had killed Sharon Tate in 1969, and it shocked the nation Cults grew from cool fads to not so cool to fads to not so good to truly just what they were. Criminals. A very unsavory fad.

Most mountain people are very cool and law-abiding, so keep to yourself. Stay in your lane, people. Don't fuck with me, and I won't fuck with your type of people, and it is highly agreed in many parts of America that this is a cool mantra. It's not about politics. It is simply about a lifestyle.

STP people were never popular, and their teepee camps with orgies and drugs and disappearances of youth continued to be a fear of law-abiding citizens, and without the beloved Sheriff, people holed up in their mountain cabins. Nederland and Eldora, Colorado side stepped. These nice people wanted nothing to do with this nonsense, fear, and lawlessness.

There were no leads to the death of the Sheriff. Everyone knew who did it. But no one knew where he fled.

No one could recall what he looked like. The STPs were a filthy group of unkempt people. It was not possible for anyone who ever met any of the men to identify the men individuals in a lineup.

The women were unique and actually pretty.

The men were filthy, ugly, unidentifiable. If they ever were clean-shaven businessmen, no one would have ever connected the dots.

Chapter 5

Due to refueling delays, the hijacked plane did not take off from Seattle until 7:40 p.m. on November 24, 1971. Most people were uniting with family for Thanksgiving the next morning. It was generally not a big media day other than college football. But a hijacking was unheard of, and so it, of course, made a gigantic splash.

Two F-106 Air Force jets and a Lock head T-33 followed in an S formation but remained out of sight.

Within 30 minutes, Cooper demanded that the aft staircase be lowered, and he wanted the airline attendant to do it. She said that the only way she would was if she was tethered to the plane.

He cut up one of the four parachutes to tether her. But in the end, he did not want to harm her. So, he deployed the aft stairs himself after he allowed her to go to the cockpit.

Chapter 6

Nederland is a tiny mountain town. This loss of the Sheriff left a family without a father, a wife without a husband, parents without a son, and siblings without a brother.

This crime was confusing and not without a giant sigh of community grief. No one would ever be the same.

Chapter 7

Around 8:00 p.m., a cockpit warning sensor lit up, indicating that the aft staircase had been deployed. The captain used the airline intercom to inquire if the hijacker needed assistance. Cooper used the shortest word in the English dictionary. "No."

At 8:13 p.m., the aircraft tail suddenly pitched forward, and the captain and crew had to use trim to correct the pitch. Their ears were popping due to a loss in cabin pressure, and it was difficult to communicate, but they knew that the aircraft was in trouble. They were flying at a low altitude at a low speed, with the aft stairwell deployed during inclement weather, and the landing gear was down on a Boeing 727. It was dark and the night before Thanksgiving and all six of them were gravely concerned that they would never see their families again.

They were somewhere near the Oregon border, and it would be a few hours at this altitude and speed before they were to refuel in Reno, Nevada.

At 11:02 p.m., they landed the plane in Reno with the aft staircase deployed. It was a firework show as the staircase hit the tarmac before the landing gear, but they managed to land the aircraft safely.

An emergency response crew was waiting for them.

FBI agents, state troopers, sheriff deputies, and Reno police encircled the plane, and it was believed that the hijacker and his bomb were still on board, so they did not approach the airplane until the captain confirmed that Cooper and the bomb were not on board.

Chapter 8

The funeral for the Nederland Sheriff was attended by hundreds of people from not only Colorado but from neighboring states as well. He was a well-known citizen of Nederland and prior to that, Boulder, and prior to that he worked in Denver and Colorado Springs.

His wife wore her police uniform, and their two sons wore their sheriff Halloween costumes from the year prior. Men and women in uniform were plentiful, but also plentiful were citizens paying their last respects.

His ashes were spread at the top of the Fourth of July Trailhead on the Continental Divide in the mountains above Nederland and Eldora, Colorado. Many people did the challenging hike to the top and it was a clear, crisp day and one could see Granby Lake as well as the Maroon Bells of Aspen.

There was not a dry eye among the crowd when the Sheriff's sister sang Amazing Grace and St. Rita's Catholic Church in Nederland.

Meanwhile, Deputy Dawg remained on the lam. The STP cult disappeared from the Nederland area after the murder. They knew that they were persona non grata in these parts, and it is believed that they migrated West to join up with the Charles Manson group.

Good riddance was the collective opinion of the citizens of Colorado.

The people were tired of the drugs and the hippies and the parties and the filthy people who felt that they were entitled to free-load and litter and clutter the streets.

The folks did not miss the illicit drugs leaked to their minor children, and they didn't miss the intoxicated miscreants roaming the streets of Boulder or Nederland or any other city or town.

Chapter 9

The forensic team had their work cut out for them when scouring the aircraft for evidence to identify D. B. Cooper. This guy was a ghost who vanished into thin air and did not leave a lot behind. The FBI team found only four pieces of evidence: a black clip-on tie, a mother-of-pearl tie clip, one hair with the follicle intact, and eight filter-tipped Raleigh cigarette butts from the armrest ashtray. This was not much to go on.

There was no fingerprint evidence and without it, DNA was scarce. Forensics was not nearly as advanced as in 1971 as it is today and so one hair follicle on the headrest was not enough to identify a man that seemed to appear out of nowhere like a magician.

Security measures were loose at airports in 1971 without radar detectors and one did not even need an identification card to purchase an airline ticket or to board the plane. For all the FBI knew, his name could have been anything.

The ticket was in the name of Dan Cooper and there were literally thousands of Dan Coopers in the United States, let alone the world. They knew that they could not assume Dan Cooper was even his name.

The FBI determined that the black clip-on tie was from a JC Penny department store, but it had not been sold in any store since 1968, so there would be no evidence of a recent purchase.

In modern years and due to the fact that this remains an unsolved crime, additional forensic analysis continues on the four pieces of evidence left behind.

It has been determined that the tie had Lycopodium spores after analyzing it with electron microscopy and identified unalloyed titanium on the tie, along with particles of bismuth, antimony, cerium, strontium sulfide, aluminum, and titanium-antimony alloys. Such rare-earth metals suggest that Cooper may have worked for Boeing or a competitor of Boeing in the aeronautical field.

The cigarette butts did not reveal any fingerprints, and current DNA analysis is impossible as these items were destroyed from the evidence locker in Las Vegas.

Chapter 10

The case went cold, and Cooper remained either on the lam or dead. Many believed that he was dead because they did not feel that it was possible that he could have successfully parachuted out of the back of the 727, flying at 10,000 carrying nearly 20 pounds of U.S. Currency with two parachutes.

But that is, in fact, what he did. If he survived, it is guessed that he landed somewhere in Southern Washington or Northern Oregon.

If he survived the jump, then he was on the lam since November 24, 1971. And then something peculiar happened. On February 10, 1980, eight-year-old Brian Ingram was vacationing with his family on the Columbia River at a beach known as Tena Bar about nine miles downstream of Vancouver, Washington. As Brian was raking the sand to build a campfire with his father, he uncovered three packets of the ransom cash, amounting to approximately $5,800.

The bills were badly weathered due to the length of exposure to the elements, but they were still bundled with rubber bands from 1971. FBI forensics confirmed that these in fact were some of the bills delivered to Cooper on November 24, 1971, at Sea-Tac International Airport.

This discovery led to more questions than answers.

It was assumed that the money made it to the ground due to gravity, and the location made sense as it was on the flight path of the Boeing 727 Flight 305 from Seattle to Mexico City. However, it did not make sense that the money had not been spent, which led the detectives to believe that Cooper was dead. His remains were never found or recovered, which also raised questions about his survival.

The Army Corps of Engineers hydrologist noted that the bills were rounded in their disintegration and matted together, suggesting that the river or one of its tributaries had carried the bills to this beach.

It made sense to forensics that he landed near the Washougal River, upstream of the Columbia River, and that the bills had made their way down to the beach. But what troubled the team was that despite being bundled in what appeared to be the original rubber bands, several of the bills were missing in the middle of the bundle. In addition, if these bundles had been in the water for nine years, the rubber bands would have disintegrated years prior.

The Army Corps of Engineers forensic hydrology team made it clear that these bills could not have arrived at Tena Beach prior to 1974 due to a dredging project that they had undertaken at that time.

Therefore, the forensic teams collectively assumed that something had changed with the status of the whereabouts of the ransom money after the summer of 1974. They just did not know the answer.

Chapter 11

Two parachutes of the four were found on the plane after it landed in Reno. One was a front parachute, and one was a rear, but one of them had been gutted, and it was presumed that Cooper had used the shell as a money bag to tether to his body when he jumped from the plane.

It is impossible to know whether the jump from the aircraft at 10,000 with 20 pounds of cash strapped to his body allowed D. B. Cooper to survive. However, if he did, he has never been seen since.

Chapter 12

It wasn't a secret that Mary MacIntosh had no love lost for the Sheriff in Sheridan, Wyoming. Mac was the prosecutor in the darling western town of northern Wyoming, and she had to deal with law enforcement at all times.

Mac had been a lawyer in Jackson Hole and then Sheridan for over 20 years and after a major criminal incident in her personal life involved her college roommates at Mac's cabin in the Rocky Mountains, she decided to take a government job prosecuting criminals.

Mac was a tall, lean, athletic, intelligent woman and she had been married once, divorced, and had no children. Her career had always come first. She didn't make time to date, and it wasn't that there weren't plenty of men who tried, but she just wasn't interested in the hassle of dating.

However, in the past year, she had prosecuted a female serial killer who wreaked havoc at several Wyoming rodeos, and she had become acquainted with a sheriff from Cheyenne, Wyoming, who helped her with the case. Sheriff Burgess was a true Wyoming cowboy sheriff, and he loved the outdoors and hunted and fished and was divorced with grown kids.

He was smitten with Mac and had been for some time, so when the opportunity knocked and he could help her resolve the female serial killer case, he made hay and showed up unexpectedly at the cabin she was enjoying in the mountains after the trial.

She answered his knock on the cabin door and to his surprise, she invited him in, and they had been dating steadily ever since. The only real challenge was that they lived about five hours from one another, and they both were busy professionals, but they did see each other whenever they were able.

They agreed on most things and one of these items was their mutual dislike for the sheriff in Sheridan. Sheriff Kane was lazy, and he was not a true officer of the law in that he really did not care about victims of crime. He showed up for work and did the bare minimum, and if it wasn't for his staff of fellow officers, the department would have a giant stain on it.

However, he was fortunate that his crew was made up of excellent women and men who went above and beyond the call of duty, and the people of Sheridan respected this team highly.

Mac and Burg did not.

Chapter 13

Author Ernest Hemingway's impact on American literature is well known, but it is especially regarding with folks from Sheridan, Wyoming. Hemingway loved Wyoming and he spent quite a bit of time in Wyoming as a writer and as a man. He loved to trout fish and hunt wild game, and he also loved the peace and tranquility of Wyoming and spent a lot of time in and near Sheridan writing his novels.

In the summer of 1928, he searched for solitude in the Rocky Mountains to write, and he landed at the Folly Ranch. He retreated to this pristine ranch outside of Sheridan, Wyoming, because he felt the calling of the quiet to finish his novel, *A Farewell to Arms*.

Hemingway was a social man, and he enjoyed his cocktails and lively chatter, but he also loved his craft, and he could not easily balance his desire to drink with the locals and finish writing a novel. He thought that the Folly Ranch would be the perfect retreat to finish this work. However, he found himself intensely annoyed by the tourists at the dude ranch that would not leave him alone. He, therefore, packed up and sequestered in Sheridan at The Sheridan Inn, which was and still is considered one of the finest hotels west of the Mississippi.

Hemingway was able to find the solitude that he desired and needed at The Sheridan Inn, but he was also within walking distance of the Sheridan WYO Theater, which was known as the Lotus at that time. The Lotus was famous at that time for its Vaudeville acts and also for the early motion picture. Many affectionately referred to this theater as Wyoming's Wonder Picture Palace, as it was home to some famous performers since its opening in 1923.

Sheridan was known for its famous dude ranchers, but it was also famous for theater as some of the first "talkies" were shown in 1929, and hundreds flocked to Sheridan to watch. And into the 1930's when Sheridan grew on the map for its dude ranches, it was crowned also as the "Western Theater for Western People." This attracted the attention of the wealthy, who wanted the authenticity of the West with the comfort of the East.

Hemingway loved his distractions from the theater to the bars, and he loved two of the most famous bars in the Sheridan area, The Mint Bar and the Last Chance Saloon. He was attempting to finish *A Farewell to Arms* during Prohibition, and it was his time at what was known as The Mint Cigar Company and Soda Shop with a speakeasy run in the back room that saved him from the Prohibition and likely allowed him what he needed to complete one of his finest works of fiction.

Hemingway was also fond of the Last Chance Saloon in Bighorn, Wyoming, which is a quintessential small sister town to Sheridan, nestled in the crook of the Bighorn Mountains a few miles away. The name referenced the fact that it was one's last chance to find a drink before heading up the treacherous switchback dirt road toward not only Folly Ranch but also one of Heminway's favorites, Spear-O-Wigwam, another dude ranch in the mountains above Sheridan.

Bighorn is a small unincorporated community in Sheridan County, Wyoming. It is home to ranching and has a large polo field. Before European settlers arrived, the area around Bighorn was inhabited by Native American tribes, including the Crow, Cheyenne, and Sioux. The Bighorn Mountains were a vital part of their territory. The town was established in the late 19th century, around the 1880s, during the western expansion of the United States.

It was primarily a ranching community benefiting from the rich grazing lands of the region. The community developed as settlers moved in, building homes, schools, and businesses.

Ranching has been a cornerstone of Bighorn's economy, and cattle and sheep continue to be crucial to the area.

Like many towns in the West, the arrival of the railroad played a significant role. Although Bighorn itself was not a railroad hub, the nearby town of Sheridan became an important stop, facilitating transportation and trade.

The Last Chance Saloon has had a few names changes over the years and one of them is Just LeDoux It Steak-Out and Saloon, named after a famous Wyoming Frontier cowboy from Cheyenne, Wyoming. The new owner rebranded under the name of the Last Chance, and it remains in this adorable original spot-on Johnson Street in Bighorn.

Hemingway loved his cocktails, and he was also a voracious carnivore and having a saloon with hard drink and red meat made him a happy man. He did in fact finish his first draft of A Farewell to Arms in Sheridan, Wyoming and he was often quoted for saying, "There are two places I love: Africa and Wyoming."

Chapter 14

Mac and Burg often met at the Last Chance Saloon on his way from Cheyenne to Sheridan to see her. They loved the small-town feel of Bighorn, Wyoming, and they did not want to be seen at the local watering holes in Sheridan. She was the prosecuting attorney, and he was a sheriff from a town of Wyoming's capital, and it was best if they kept their private lives private to the extent that they were able. However, the Last Chance Saloon had the best steak in town, and they both loved a good steak and a great whiskey.

While sitting there enjoying dinner in a back booth, in walks the sheriff from Sheridan. Mac outwardly groaned.

"Kane is here," she motioned to Burg. He turned slightly to see Sheriff Kane.

"Great. The lazy bastard probably will expect me to buy him a drink," Burg replied.

"Don't make eye contact," Mac urged Burg.

"Too late. He's on his way over."

"Well, look at what we have here," Sheriff Kane said. "If it isn't the two love birds."

Mac wanted to kick him in the shin.

"How's it going, Kane?" Burg asked.

"Another day, another dollar," Kane replied.

Mac had a thought bubble that would have read something like, "All you do is collect taxpayer's money without giving a rat's ass about public safety," but of course, she kept her mouth shut.

"I thought you lived on the other side of town," Burg said to Kane.

"I do, but the wife would find out if I were downtown, so I sneak out here for some peace and quiet," Kane said.

Mac rolled her eyes. She couldn't help herself. Burg nudged her knee under the table.

"Come join us," Burg said. Kane immediately took a seat next to Mac. Now, she wanted to kick Burg. "I am up for a few days, and I am trying to convince Mac to go tent camping with me, but she is balking at the possibility of a change in the weather. She's usually tougher than this, so it costs me a filet and a whiskey or two."

Kane smirked. She hated it when he smirked. He looked coy. "She's a tough nut to crack," Kane said, poking Mac in her arm as he said it. She hated that, too. She wanted to rear back and throat punch him.

They continued to chat, and Burg bought Kane a drink but after he finished it, Mac informed Kane that she and Burg were going home to figure out their weekend plans.

Chapter 15

Mac and Burg agreed to the camping and fishing weekend, and together, they loaded Burg's truck with both of their gear and headed up the Red Grade of the Bighorn Mountains.

The road in the Bighorn Mountains is called the "Red Grade" due to the reddish color of the soil and rock formations that are characteristic of the area. The term "grade" often refers to a slope or incline in a road, so "Red Grade" describes both the color and nature of the terrain. The red color comes from the iron-rich rocks and soil commonly found in the Bighorn Mountains, which have oxidized to give them a red hue.

They drove to Dead Swede Campground and set up their tent and supplies at a campsite near the creek. They both loved campsite cooking, and they set about oiling the cast iron pan so that when they brought back some rainbow trout from their fishing expedition, they could fry them for dinner.

Burg was a fly fisherman, while Mac preferred to cast out from shore. She could see Burg a way upstream standing in the middle of the creek in his wader boots, a vest with flies and tie offs and tools, and a floppy hat. She loved to watch him flick his wrist while casting with such grace and ease.

Burg's technique was Nymph casting using weighted flies that sink below the surface, imitating aquatic insects in their larval stage. This technique was best for trout feeding underwater. Often the fisherman uses and indicator to detect subtle bites and adjust weight and depth according to water conditions.

As Mac was watching Burg, she felt a strong tug on her line. She was using worms, and apparently, she had a bite. She started reeling in, keeping her rod high and not reeling too quickly. She could see the Rainbow fighting, and she knew it was a beauty. The hues of pinks, purples, and greens sinewed in the rays of sunshine on the water, and as she pulled this 22-inch fish in, she admired its beauty.

As she pulled the hook out of its gills and slid it on her line to leave it in the water to stay fresh for cooking, she heard a voice behind her.

She turned to see an older man standing there watching her. She waved hello. He waved back.

"What were you using as bait," he said. He was wearing old clothing that looked like it had not been washed in months, and he had stringy, long grey hair and a patchy beard. His shoes were worn thin, and his fingernails were long and uneven.

"Worms," she responded. She noticed that he had his rod in hand, and she motioned with her head toward her canister of worms. Try a few of mine. They are fresh. Just got 'em today," she said.

He approached timidly at first and fumbled in the dirt to pull out a long, squirming worm, which he pierced on his hook. She watched him cast out into the creek. She dug out a worm, too, and she cast beside him.

He reeked of body odor. "Do you live up here?" she asked. He nodded in the affirmative.

"Year-round?" Again, he nodded yes. "Must be freezing in the winter." He nodded in agreement. He was a man of few words.

"Hey, my friend and I are going to catch a few more trout and fry them at that campsite over there," Mac said to the man, motioning her head in the direction of their tent. "Would love for you to join us."

The man did not say a word. He simply walked downstream with his fishing line still in the creek.

Mac watched this old man walk away, and she surmised that he must be in his 70s, living off the land. Wyoming winters were harsh, especially in the mountains, and she hoped that he had some kind of shelter to keep him warm. Everything about him was in tatters, and he was extremely unkempt. It was unusual sitting in this area where most people knew each other, and if someone offered hospitality, it was customary to take it. It was an odd encounter, for sure. She was looking forward to telling Burg about it back at their campsite.

Chapter 16

The FBI officially closed the case on D. B. Cooper on July 8, 2016. After 45 years of investigation with no conclusive leads, the FBI decided to allocate resources to other investigations.

The case remains one of the greatest unsolved mysteries in U.S. history, with the identity and fate of D. B. Cooper still unknown.

Chapter 17

"Who were you talking with while fishing," Burg asked as they were frying their trout and sipping on a whiskey.

"Some old man who did not talk a single word. He just nodded to my questions, and when I asked if he wanted to join us for dinner, he left," Mac said.

"Um. Odd."

"And get this. I think he lives here year-round off the grid, and I'm not sure about shelter. He is probably 70 or 75, and he was extremely unkempt."

"Harsh environment to live here in the winter," Burg replied. Mac nodded in agreement.

Mac and Burg fried their trout in the cast iron pan that Mac had inherited from a family she never met. They sat by their campfire and sipped their Jameson, and talked into the night.

Chapter 18

No need for an alarm clock with either Mac or Burg. They both slept like logs and woke at 6:30 a.m. Clockwork. She got up in the middle of the night to pee, but he did not. She did not snore unless she was very tired, and he always did. She slept on her back and did not move. He slept willy-nilly and tossed and turned all night, and if on his back, the Pacific Northern Railroad was quieter.

But they managed to sleep well together. It was their connection. She loved to be held. He loved to hold her. Their love language was not gifts. It was a physical connection, and this wasn't only about sex. It was about their hearts, minds, bodies, and the universe connecting as they lay in one another's arms, and for them, it worked.

Burg had been married and divorced and had two kids. Mac had never had kids, as she spent her time working.

She loved kids, and she loved spending time with Burg and his now adult kids and when his oldest announced that he and his wife were going to have a baby, Burg was over the moon.

This prompted in his mind "the talk." He wanted to talk with Mac about marriage. They had never discussed it.

They just went with the flow and saw one another when they could, but nothing was more than the here and now.

Once Burg learned that he was going to be a Papa, he didn't want to be Papa and his girlfriend. He wanted to be Papa and Mama. Grandma. Grandma Mary.

This was the impetus for the camping trip. Mac had no clue that this was their Saturday morning conversation over campsite coffee. But Burg had planned this out.

He knew that if he could get her in the mountains where she loved to be, and if he could fry her fresh trout and they could sleep under the stars and make love to her favorite soft music and giggle into the night like teens, he could prompt the question. And that is precisely what he did.

It was early, and the sun was rising, but he had barely slept a wink. He waited patiently as she slept, but as she started to stir with the morning light, he positioned himself in their joint sleeping bag with a ring in his hand and a question on his mind.

They had only been together for nine months. They had known each other for a few years professionally, but not well. They had always locked eyes at professional gatherings, but Mac was always busy and in her own head, and she really didn't give men the time of day. She was so into the practice of law that she forgot about the practice of love.

She took great care of herself physically and kept in great shape both mentally and physically, but emotionally, she ignored herself and others.

Burg was the opposite. He took great care of other people, and he ignored his physique. He was in good enough condition to hike with the best of them, but he had a belly, and he was a tad weathered from the summer sun.

Mac didn't care about his belly. She liked the fact that she could melt into him with a hug and fall asleep on a dime in his arms. Burg loved that she did this, and he loved her firm athletic build. It worked for them.

On this fine early summer morning in the mountains of the Bighorns off the Red Grade, Mac stirred. She opened her brown eyes, stretched her arms over her head, and made her squeaky morning stretch. "let's take on this day" noise that Burg had grown to tolerate.

She was on her back in their dual sleeping bag that she had bought them when she learned that he loved to tent camp. She admitted to being a body heat mooch and cuddler, so he was thrilled with the only gift she had ever given him. It was something useful that they could enjoy together.

As she awoke, she opened her eyes to see him on his left side, staring at her. He seemed intense. Or tense. This was unusual.

The traditional Irish wedding band is known as the Claddagh ring, which has a rich history and symbolism rooted deeply in Irish culture.

The Claddagh ring features three main elements: a heart (symbolizing love), a pair of hands (symbolizing friendship), and a crown (symbolizing loyalty). Together, these elements symbolize love, friendship, and loyalty, which are the tenements of a good relationship.

Mac and Burg had never discussed marriage and therefore, he had no idea of what to present her at the moment of proposal. She did not know much about her family due to its fractured nature. But he knew her strong bond with her Irish heritage, and Burg was Scott-Irish, and he knew that symbolism of the Claddagh. He made a decision not to go with the traditional fancy diamond. He went with symbolism.

The Claddagh ring originated in the fishing village of Claddagh, near Galway, Ireland, where Mac's father's family was from. The design is attributed to Richard Joyce, a silversmith who, according to Irish legend, was captured by pirates and sold into slavery in Algeria, Africa. During his time in captivity, he honed the craft of jewelry-making and crafted the first Claddagh ring for his fiancée back in Ireland. Upon his release, he returned to his native Galway and presented her with his gift of a Claddagh ring made specifically for her, symbolizing his unending love and loyalty.

The Claddagh ring is worn to symbolize the status of a relationship. It can be marriage or friendship. The manner in which it is worn it the ticker. On the right hand with the heart facing outward, the wearer is single.

On the right hand with the heart facing inward, the wearer is in a relationship. On the left hand with the heart facing outward, the wearer is engaged. On the left hand, with the heart facing inward, the wearer is married.

The Claddagh ring has grown to be a popular symbol in Irish heritage and is often passed down through generations as a family heirloom. Burg was holding his grandmother's ring in his right hand when Mac awoke. He watched her affectionately as she stirred. He had already been up to relieve himself and to make her his infamously wonderfully strong camp side coffee, and the tent smelled of the morning in the mountains with freshly brewed coffee.

Their eyes locked as he lay on his side. He looked intense, which was unusual for this laid-back man. She always had an air of intensity, but she was in the mountains in nature next to the only man she had ever loved, and her look was natural and soft.

"Good morning, Sunshine," he greeted her day.

"Morning," she replied, still waking up in a sleepy tone.

She noted that he was quieter than normal. He was a human chatterbox and would normally be espousing their plans for the day. But not this Saturday. He was simply gazing at her. It made her nervous. She rolled to her side near him.

"What's up?" she asked.

"You, finally," he responded.

It was early. It wasn't like she slept in and wrecked his weekend plans. It confused her.

"What time is it?"

"It's 6:30," he said.

This was their normal routine. No alarms. They usually both stirred around 6:30. But his look said that he had been waiting for her to wake up for hours. It was accurate.

"I have something I have been meaning to ask you," Burg stated in a very serious tone. It concerned her. He was normally not so intense unless it was regarding work.

"Ok. What's up?" Mac asked.

"What's up is that I love you, and I don't want to die alone," was his ever-so-romantic segue.

She giggled. There he was. Burg was a romantic klutz. She wanted to inquire, but she felt like he was not finished.

"I would be honored if you would be my wife." He handed her his grandmother's Claddagh ring. It was simple and silver and a tad tarnished, and her heart skipped several beats. He was quiet again, awaiting a response.

"It would be my honor and privilege," Mac said.

Needless to say, the Saturday hike to the Continental Divide could wait.

Chapter 19

The hike to the Continental Divide was hard and long, and Mac couldn't wait to dip into the creek upon returning to the campground. She knew that she smelled like sweat. Burg loved her au natural fragrance, but she did not love his. She convinced him to take a skinny dip with her.

As they dried off and dressed, Mac sensed that they were being watched. She looked around but did not see another soul. They needed to fish again for dinner, so they got their poles, and Burg waded upstream to fly fish; she hovered near the campsite and cast her line. It was late afternoon, and the fish were jumping, and it wasn't long before she landed her first catch. Burg was always in awe that she was so lucky with a cast. She had natural instincts and was not reluctant to dig for a big earthworm as bait. Each would squirm and twist around her fingers when she baited her hook, and she was not squeamish about the process.

He continued his way upstream, searching for the perfect fishing hole, when she caught glimpses of movement downstream on the other side of the creek. It was the old man again. He wasn't trying to hide from her. He actually nodded in her direction. He wasn't a man of words, but they made eye contact. She waved at him, but he did not wave back.

She held up her first catch to show him, and he nodded. What she had imagined was a congratulatory nod.

He had his pole as well, and she motioned for him to join her. He stayed put and cast his line and was soon lucky as well. The fish were hungry. So was Mac.

She glanced down at the Claddagh ring on her left ring finger and sighed to herself. They were going to get married. They spoke of it at length during their hike and how to handle it logistically. Burg had a great job as the Sheriff in Cheyenne, and she loved being County Prosecutor in Sheridan. It was a six-to-seven-hour drive, depending on road conditions. Sometimes, Interstate 25 was closed in the winter, making it impossible to see one another during a blizzard.

They were going to need to noodle this one a lot. Cheyenne was near the Wyoming/Colorado border, making flights from Denver easy, but they didn't travel often. Sheridan was much more beautiful as it is a quintessential darling western town nestled at the base of the Bighorn Mountains as part of the Rocky Mountain chain. Outdoor activities were abundant, and they both were active outdoor enthusiasts. Sheridan was the natural answer for where to join households. The only real hurdle was Burg's job.

Chapter 20

Mac was back at work early Monday morning. Burg had left at the crack of dawn from Sheridan to drive back to Cheyenne for his shift. She looked at her ring finger affectionally and was admiring the Claddagh ring when her assistant poked her head in to tell her that her nine-thirty appointment was waiting for her.

"Oh! What's that on your hand," Christine asked.

"It's Burg's grandmother's Claddagh ring. He popped the question while we were camping this past weekend," Mac replied.

"And I assume you said yes?"

"Yes! Other than the logistics of where to live, we are both thrilled."

"I vote for Sheridan," Christine said.

"Me too, and Burg does as well. We just need to figure out his work situation. There are no openings for a sheriff in Sheridan, despite the fact that Sheriff Kane barely does his job."

Christine rolled her eyes and nodded in agreement. "He's worthless and a royal asshole," she said,

"Speaking of, Burg and I were at the Last Chance when he was out, and we were having dinner and drinks when Kane sauntered in like he owned the place. Of course, Burg asked him to join us for a drink.

I almost killed him for the offering. Anyway, Kane was his usual asshole self and even had the nerve to poke me when talking to me. He's lucky that I didn't throat-punch him. I was close to doing it, but my job requires that I not commit crimes," Mac joked.

She was serious about her desire to throat-punch him, though Christine probably knew. Not many people in town like Kane, and Mac does not hold back on her opinion of him when talking to people in her inner circle.

"He's always at the Last Chance. I guess it's because his wife would find out if he were at a local watering hole in Sheridan, so he sneaks over to Bighorn to avoid getting caught," Christine said. Mac nodded.

"You can send in my 9:30 appointment. I need to get this day started," Mac said. Christine understood and swiftly left to get her appointment from the lobby.

Chapter 21

Mac had a number of trials coming up, and she had a very busy week of work, most days ending around dinner but starting at sun-up. She usually did her morning run around five and then was at the office by seven. She had her hands full with prosecuting mostly minor felonies. The crime rate was fortunately relatively low in Sheridan. Most crimes involved drugs or alcohol.

And prosecuting also involved good police work and Lord knows that Sheriff Kane did not offer that to her. His sloppy detective work made her job much more difficult, but luckily, Kane had good assistants in his force that did good investigatory work.

Mac's cell phone rang around nine in the evening, and she was home in bed binge-watching reruns of Gilmore Girls when she answered. It was Burg on the line, and he sounded plussed.

"Did you hear the news?" he asked in a heightened tone.

"No. What news," Mac asked.

"Kane has been shot and killed at the Last Chance Saloon tonight. About an hour ago," Burg said.

"Oh my God. Why? How? What happened?" she asked. Her heart was now racing, and she quickly hopped out of bed and switched the programming to the local news.

Sure enough, it was all over the news that Sheriff Kane was sitting at the bar in Bighorn having a beer after work, and some random older guy was popping off to him. Kane apparently didn't like it, but he didn't feel like getting into it. The guy followed Kane out to his patrol car and shot him in the back of the head execution style and the older guy walked away into the dark, and no one knew who he was or where he went.

Mac was reporting what she was hearing on the news to Burg. He already knew the facts, but he listened to her anyway.

"I heard a ton of sirens about an hour ago, but they faded, so I didn't think much of it," Mac said to Burg.

"It was probably in response to this," Burg suggested.

"They have no idea who did this?" Mac asked.

"None. At first, people thought that it was a guy on drugs or drunk, but witnesses at the Last Chance reported that this guy was sober, and no one had ever seen him before," Burg said.

"Do you think that it was someone that he arrested at some point," Mac asked.

"It's possible. No one knows, and no one has ever seen this guy before. Witnesses are giving statements as we speak, and the composite artist is out in Bighorn at the Last Chance, drawing this guy's likeness for display on the news and in town. The renditions should be available within the hour," Burg reported.

Mac and Burg ended their call, and Mac started making calls to the police force to see if she could get updated information. A female officer responded with a screenshot of the artist's rendition of the killer. He had a strong jaw, big ears, narrowly set brown eyes, and a wide forehead. His hair was scraggly and unkempt, and his skin was weathered. Mac was utterly astonished to see the face of the old man that she fished next to at the campground over the weekend. The man who didn't speak. He killed Sheriff Kane, and Mac knew where he lived.

Mac shared the screenshot with Burg and told him that it was the guy at the campground. Burg never saw the old man up close, but he trusted his now fiancée. Mac was bright, and attention to detail never escaped her. He called her again.

"Is that the guy?" Burg asked her.

"Absolutely. It's him. I can't imagine why he would kill Kane. But I'm positive that he is the guy," Mac said.

"Have you told anyone?"

"Not yet."

"What are you going to do?"

"I am going to call my contact at the police station and my contact on the news, and I will request an APD for a search of the Bighorn Mountains, specifically in the area where we camped. Who knows where he went after he did this, but we need to find this man."

"It's too dark to fly a copter up the mountain," Burg said.

"I know, but at least they can send out crew for a land search tonight and then launch aerial tomorrow at Sunup."

"Right. I will call Stan. He can get the copters in Douglas ready to go," Burg said.

Chapter 22

The minute the sun was up, illuminating the Bighorn Mountains, Stan had his crew up in the air on a search for the killer.

Stan was a good friend of Burg and was part of the law enforcement team that flew the helicopters when searching for criminals or things as simple as someone lost in a snowstorm in the mountains. He was a well-qualified certified pilot, and Burg trusted Stan with his life when up in the air.

Burg gave Stan the coordinates to the campground in the Bighorn Mountains, and Stan assured Burg that the two-helicopter search crew would leave no inch of the mountain unsearched.

Meanwhile, in Sheridan, the town was once again in shock. It was only a few months ago that the female serial killer ravaged the Sheridan WYO Rodeo and killed five local teens. Now this violent crime was rare in this part of the woods, and two violent criminals in one year were upending this close-knit community. Despite the fact that Sheriff Kane was not widely liked, he was a public servant, and he was not a bad guy. His family was mourning the loss of their son, husband, father, uncle, etc., and no one could understand why this happened.

When the owner of the Last Chance Saloon was interviewed regarding the incidents that led up to the murder, Jessica Winner stated that she was working behind the bar as a bartender, and she served Kane whiskey. The old man was tucked at the end of the bar, drinking a Bourbon and 7-Up, and was glaring at Kane, who was still in uniform. Jessica noticed tension. She knew Kane well as he was a regular, but she had never seen this old man before, and she was curious as to why he was glaring at the Sheriff.

She described the scenario to law enforcement and explained that at some point, the old man popped off to the Sheriff unprovoked, and Kane ignored him at first. But after his second drink, the old man upped to provocation and was growing belligerently rude.

Kane did not know this guy, but instinctually, Kane knew that this dude could be armed. He looked suspicious and mean, and Kane was in no mood for an altercation. He hadn't had the best day at the office, and he was about to go home to a chaotic household with an unhappy wife and unruly teens.

But the tension was building as this man continued and finally, Kane had had enough. He finished his drink and paid Jessica the bill and he got up to leave. As he walked out the front door of the Last Chance Saloon, the old man followed, and the next thing Jessica heard with a single gunshot.

Everyone in the bar ran out to see what happened, and Kane was lying in a pool of blood, face down and alone. The old man was nowhere to be seen.

Chapter 23

The manhunt continued for days to no avail. This old man was a ghost. He was nowhere near the campsite where Mac and Burg saw him, and he was nowhere to be found.

Mac was again under pressure to figure out who this person was, and the police force was caught in the vortex of investigating a crime, mourning their leader, and not having a leader.

City Council needed to appoint an interim sheriff, and it made sense to have a local police officer currently on staff to step in for now. They appointed Jennifer Saxton to lead the force in not only the search but also cleaning up what Kane left behind, which was a lot of work as he was lazy.

Mac was dreading going to Kane's funeral that week. She had not been to a funeral since she lost Harry, her boss, a few years prior, and she was not looking forward to drudging up the feelings of loss. However, she loved Harry with her heart and soul. He was her father, for all intents and purposes. Losing him to lung cancer was horrible. Watching it was horrible. A giant of a man shrinks to nothing. Like John Wayne. True Grit.

Kane's funeral would be sad, but mostly for his loved ones. Burg was allowed a PTO day to attend as were most law enforcement officers in the state. The good news was that Burg would be up again the next weekend, and they could have time to plan their wedding. Burg wanted to get married soon. He did not want to wait. Mac was fine either way, and she decided to let him set the pace.

"That was a nice service," Mac said to Burg as they left the church the next Friday morning.

"It was, but it was hard to look at those teenage boys knowing that they lost their father," Burg said.

"I need to go back to the office and work," Mac said. He understood that he needed to check in with his staff. She set him up in a conference room, and he was able to do what he needed to while she did what she had planned.

Chapter 24

Burg reported that Stan and his team were still searching for the old man via air and land but that nothing had proven fruitful thus far. It was frustrating. It was like he was a ghost and vanished into thin air.

In the meantime, he sheepishly approached the Sheriff's Department and City Council and applied to become Sheridan County Sheriff. He had not even told Mac about doing so, but he did it Monday morning before he drove back to Cheyenne. It wasn't like he was keeping a secret from her, but somehow, he rationalized that if he told her and she got her hopes up and he didn't get the position, she would be disappointed. He didn't want that to be the case. She was so impressed with him, and she seemed to manage life-challenging moments with gusto. She overcame so many obstacles in her life and came through on the other side shining. She was fearless. He was not.

He feared failure. She took it on as a challenge. Her motto was something to the effect of "a closed door is an open window." That exemplified her manner of dealing with issues.

Mac was busy preparing for trial in a case of cattle and sheep rustling.

Two men had been stealing livestock in Sheridan County and the four ranchers who had been the victims of this were piping mad and wanted reimbursement and justice. Therefore, Mac was deep in depositions and interrogatories to prepare for the upcoming trial before Judge Maurita Redle.

She was also behind in a dental appointment with Dr. Michelle Meehan and, therefore, had scheduled an early morning appointment for the first of October for a routine cleaning. Dr. Meehan had her office near the fairgrounds of the Sheridan WYO Rodeo, and it was close to where Mac lived. She was able to pop in for her appointment before work. Dr. Meehan's daughter, Gabby, was in high school and contemplating dental school and, therefore, was helping in the office before school. Mac had the pleasure of meeting this young whippersnapper of a teenager who was bright and driven like the doc's mother.

When she got to the office, there was a message from her assistant that Stan had called to update her on the air and ground search for the old man. She promptly returned his call.

"Nothing yet," Stan said. "We will keep at it as long as we have the resources to do so."

"I will ensure that you have all of the resources that you need," Mac said. "I have spoken with the mayor and the governor, and they have committed full throttle to this."

"Good. As much as Kane was a butthole, his killer needs to be caught before this happens again. I don't understand why this man killed Kane. The eyewitnesses all agree that Kane was minding his own business at the Last Chance. It was an unprovoked killing," Stan said.

"That's what we conjecture after interviewing Jessica and everyone else in the bar that night," Mac said.

"Has Burg heard anything regarding the Sheridan Sheriff position yet," Stan inquired.

"What is Sheridan Sheriff's position," Mac asked.

There was a pregnant pause on the line. Stan quickly surmised that Burg hadn't told Mac that he had applied. The cat was out of the bag. Stan had stepped in it.

"Um. I'm sorry. I figured that you knew," Stan said.

"I knew what?"

"He applied for the job. I don't know why he didn't tell you," Stan said.

But Mac quickly figured it out. Burg didn't tell her if he did not get the position. She knew down deep that he didn't want to disappoint her. Therefore, she covered for him.

"He probably doesn't want to upset me if he doesn't land this. You know that we are engaged, right?" Mac said.

"Yes," he told me. He's so excited to marry you, and he's trying to make your worlds meld," Stan replied.

"It will work out. I just know it. But thanks for the heads up. Knowledge is power."

"We all know that you like power," Stan chided.

"Who doesn't?" Mac retorted as they ended the conversation.

Chapter 25

Mac's cell rang shortly thereafter. It was Burg. She figured that Stan would be on the horn with him the minute they ended their conversation.

"I have something to tell you," Burg said sheepishly. Mac just listened. She could have let him off the hook easily and cut to the bait, but she decided to hear him out. "I applied for the position," he said.

"I know. Best of luck. You are more than qualified. I hope that you find it. If there's anything that I can do to help, please let me know," Mac said.

"There is. If you have the chance to speak with the mayor and anyone on the City Council, that would help if you gave them the elevator pitch for me," Burg said.

"No problem. I have a call in already to the mayor regarding funding for the search for the old man who killed Kane, and I have no problem with a segue pitch on your behalf."

"Thanks."

"Thank you. You are willing to relocate for us. That means a lot to me," Mac said.

"I would do anything for you and for us," Burg replied softly but with conviction.

Chapter 26

There was a call on hold for Mac as she ended her cell conversation with Burg. When her assistant popped in to tell her that a sheriff from Boulder, Colorado, was on hold for her, she was intrigued by the call.

"This is Mary MacIntosh," she announced quite formally on the line.

"Hello. My name is Sheriff Lawrence, and I work for the Boulder County force," he said. "We heard that you had a sheriff that was killed execution-style at a small-town pub, and I wanted to share something with you in case it is helpful with your investigation," he said.

"Please. We have no leads. None. It's incredibly frustrating. This man who killed Sheriff Kane vanished into thin air. Like a ghost," Mac said.

"We had a similar case a long time ago. When I was a little kid. My dad was the sheriff in Boulder at the time, and I remember him talking to my mom about it. My parents have long passed away, so I can't ask them, but anyone who was around in the 70s in this area remembers Deputy Dawg," he said.

"Deputy Dawg?" Mac asked. She had not heard of him.

"Yes. He was part of this old hippie druggie crew that hung around Boulder and Nederland, Colorado, in the 60s and 70s, and they were not peaceful hippies.

They were a spin-off of the Charles Manson crew, and they were troublemakers. Anyway, Deputy Dawg was one of them. They all had weird monikers. his dude was in the Pioneer Inn, which is a bar in Nederland, and for no reason, this punk kid followed the sheriff out of the bar, shot him execution style, and left his remains in the woods. It was weeks before some hunters found his body, and by then, it was badly decomposed," Sheriff Lawrence explained. "He disappeared into thin air and has not been seen since. I thought that I would share this with you because the facts mirror what happened in your town."

"Interesting," Mac said. "They are highly similar. "Do you happen to have any more information regarding this Deputy Dawg character?"

"No. He has been on the lam since 1971. It is believed that he was around 19 when he killed the sheriff, so that would put him in his 70's by now. The crew lived off the land in teepees and the like, so this guy could easily survive in the mountains. That's why I called it is possible that this is your guy," Sheriff Lawrence said.

"Can you scan and send me the file if it is still around?" Mac asked. It was a cold case, and she knew it and she prayed that archives had not destroyed it.

"Already in the works," he said. We asked our archives to find it and they did, and we are scanning it and will be sending it to your assistant and to the sheriff's office in Sheridan."

"Thank you," Mac said. "Do you happen to have a sketch of this guy? We have a rendition of the killer based on eyewitnesses who were at the Last Chance, and it would be interesting to see if there is a likeness."

"It is on its way to your office as we speak," Sheriff Lawrence said.

Mac thanked him over and over again. This was good detective work, and she was ever so grateful. So far, they had no leads. This was the first.

Chapter 27

Mac called Jessica, the owner of the Last Chance Saloon, and asked her to drop by on her way to Bighorn to work to look at the composite sketch of Deputy Dawg to see if she saw a likeness in comparison to the old man that she saw in her bar. Jessica confirmed the likeness. They had a solid lead.

The sheriff's office issued an APB on "Deputy Dawg," and his composite from 1971 was combined with the current one created after Sheriff Kane was killed, and both renditions were spread on the local news in both Wyoming and Colorado. The sheriff's office phone was ringing off the hook.

There was a call waiting for Mac once again. This time it was the sheriff's office in Seattle, Washington with another lead.

"This is Mary MacIntosh," she announced on the line.

"Hello, Ms. MacIntosh, this is the Seattle police department calling to speak with you about a man by the assumed name of D. B. Cooper," Sheriff Sackett said. She filled Mac in on the details of why she was calling. Her daughter worked at the Boulder, Colorado, sheriff's office and sent her the dual composites. "I need to talk to you about an unsolved case from November 24, 1971, involving a plane hijacking," she said.

"Go on," Mac was intrigued. She remembered the name and the incident in question. A man hijacked a plane the day before Thanksgiving from Portland to Seattle and somehow, after his ransom demands were met, managed to jump from the plane and has never been seen since.

"D. B. Cooper hijacked this plane in 1971. Deputy Dawg killed the sheriff in Nederland in the summer of 1971, and these men look very, very similar to one another," Sheriff Sackett continued. "It can't just be a coincidence. Two men commit two outlandish crimes in the same year, and they look alike, and both remain on the lam."

"That is a remarkable coincidence," Mac agreed. "Tell me more about the hijacking. I remember it as a kid and it was the talk of the town over the Thanksgiving weekend, I recall."

"Oh, yes! It was the crime of the century in our neck of the woods, and in 1980, some little boy was on vacation near the mouth of the Columbia River, and he found some of the ransom money when he was raking sand to make a campfire with his dad," Sheriff Sackett continued. She filled Mac in on the details of the crime.

Chapter 28

Things were heating up around the nation now that there was a possible link between the two crimes, and the D. B. Cooper followers were now involved in the fray. D. B. Cooper fans had a cult-like following. There were fan clubs and paraphernalia for these fans who found this crime to be the crime of the century. People were in awe of him, and there were D. B. Cooper festivals for years following the hijacking.

Phones were ringing off the hook not only in Sheridan but also in every newsroom across the country. This was now the topic of the news, and the media flocked to Sheridan to be at the crux of activity.

The courthouse was swarmed with camera crews and reporters, and Mac had to use a back entrance for ingress and egress from work. They followed her home. She had to politely request some privacy; however, they flocked to her even during her early morning runs. She knew better than to get upset with them for the sake of her career, as they were just doing their jobs like she was. But she didn't appreciate the fanfare. She needed her morning runs to think clearly and plan her day. She was not allowed to do this, and it bothered her.

She called Burg on her run to vent. He listened to her patiently and promised to be there as early as possible on Friday and stay for the weekend.

He could offer some solace, and they could sneak away if that was what she needed. It was October now and cooling off Camping was dicey with weather, but they could take a road trip to Montana and hide away in a cabin, or Mac always had an open invitation to stay at Butch Anderson's cabin in the mountains if he wasn't using it.

Mac was happy that Burg would be there with her. She wanted to stay home, though. She had too much to do, and she also wanted to be around her rescue kittens, Snow, Suki, and Sampson.

They offered her companionship and comfort when she was stressed.

He understood and agreed to hunker down. He wanted to help her unpack as well. Mac recently bought a cute three-bedroom house near the fairgrounds, and she hadn't had time to unpack or to fix the small things around the home that needed fixing. Burg was handy. Mac was, too, but her time was spent at the office or working at home, and her honey-do list was piling up.

Chapter 29

If D. B. Cooper was Deputy Dawg, the identify of this man was still very unclear. No one really knew who Deputy Dawg was. The hippies that he used to associate with in the STP crew just knew him by his moniker. With regard to D. B. Cooper, he bought his plane ticket in Portland with cash, and the ticket was actually issued to Dan Cooper. The "D. B." part was a mistake made early on by a reporter. Instead of reporting on Dan Cooper, somehow, he mixed it up with D. B. Cooper, and it stuck. So, there was never a confirmation of the identification of Dan Cooper, and therefore, no one to this day can say with any certainty who he is.

He did not leave any fingerprints behind on the hijacked plane, and these two crimes happened in 1971 when CODIS was not nearly as sophisticated. Therefore, since the cigarette butts did not have fingerprints when tested in Reno and were subsequently thrown away out of the evidence locker, they could not be tested with modern technology.

Without any clue as to the true identity of either Deputy Dawg or D. B. Cooper, it was possible that these were the same men, but equally possible that they were not. The crimes committed in 1971 were completely different. One was murder for no apparent motive, and one was hijacking for a specific financial motive.

If they were linked somehow, these men seemed very unlike one another. One was a punk druggie hippie, and one was a quiet, well-organized man with a very specific plan to execute a sophisticated hijacking for ransom.

Most who knew Deputy Dawg felt that he was not intellectual enough and was too young to be D. B. Cooper. And the D. B. Cooper obsessed fan club felt the same way. They felt that Cooper was far too intellectual to be confused with a hippie of Charles Manson ilk.

Nevertheless, the media was going crazy with this story. It had legs. It had hype. It had sex appeal in that people still felt strongly about both crimes.

Therefore, it was getting a lot of nationwide attention.

Chapter 30

With the media crowding the streets of Sheridan and Bighorn and the residents of both towns trying to simply lead their normal lives, there was a growing atrophy about the case and a growing pressure on Mac to solve it so that life could return to normal in Sheridan and Bighorn.

The new leads felt promising to Mac, but they could be a giant rabbit hole. She wasn't sure. But since they were her only leads, she had to follow them.

The Deputy Dawg character made the most sense. He was the right age, and it was the same crime, and he'd been on the lam for so long. He was a mountain hippie who lived off the land, so it was a natural fit that a hippie living off the land in Colorado and who killed a sheriff would naturally matriculate north to Wyoming and become a recluse.

The D. B. Cooper part did not really fit. It was a well-thought-out hijacking, and it was on the West Coast. It was also highly possible that he did not survive the jump. The parachutes could have failed. The ransom cash could have been too heavy at nearly 20 pounds. The altitude of 10,000 feet could have proven fatal. The weather conditions, with cold temperatures and rain, could have been fatal. The lack of oxygen could have been fatal. It was so much more likely that he didn't survive than the opposite conclusion.

Some of the ransom money washed downriver on the Columbia and was discovered within a decade of the hijacking.

She had to keep an open mind about any possible lead. She had her paralegal working on it, and the Sheriff's Office was also working on it. Stan's crew was in the air and on foot searching, and, of course, Burg was working on it. He had plenty of staff to handle some of his load, and he had worked his way up over the years to manage his own time. He also had a lot of forensic contacts in the field to help. The issue on the forensic side is that there was no forensics for either crime. No identification. No fingerprints. No DNA. There is not one clue to tie either of these individuals to a certain identity or to each other. It was extremely frustrating.

Mac appreciated the support. She needed nuggets to feed to the media so that they would settle down. And she also needed the town to know that they were working 24/7 trying to solve this crime.

Chapter 31

Mac's cell phone rang. It was early and she had just finished her morning run and was showered and about to head to the office. It was Stan, so she answered quickly.

"We think we might have found something in the mountains," he said.

Her interest perked. She was sipping her strong, black coffee, and with this news, she gulped too much of the hot brew.

"What's up?" Mac asked, putting down her mug.

"We found an encampment way downriver from your campsite with Burg. It is a shanty near a cave that looks to be a place where a person might be able to survive year-round. No one is there right now, but I have a search team there, and I've called Burg. He's sending his expert forensic guy on a plane to Sheridan this morning. He will be met by a team member and taken to the encampment for forensic analysis," Stan said.

"I want to be part of it," Mac said.

"Of course, that's why Burg is on the plane with his forensic buddy. You are to meet them at the Sheridan airport and go with them up the Red Grade to the encampment."

"Roger that," Mac said. She made an about-face and changed from her business suit into jeans and a flannel shirt. She packed her backpack with warm clothes and her laptop with her solar charging device. She called the office and left a message for her assistant and her paralegal regarding her plans. She asked that they cancel her appointments for the day. Her assistant would need to make a court appearance for her before Judge Maurita Redle and ask for a continuance on an arraignment.

Extenuating circumstances had intervened, and Judge Redle would understand.

Mac met Burg and his two forensic buddies at the airport, and she drove them in her Jeep up the mountain. Burg was on the phone with Stan, and Stan sent coordinates for the homestead cave. When Burg was out of cell range as they went up the mountain, he finally turned his attention to Mac.

"Good morning, he finally said."

She gave him a sideways glance as she traversed the winding red shale road. She had both hands on the steering wheel and eyes on the road.

"Good morning to you guys as well," she finally said.

Chapter 32

As they got closer to the coordinates for the cave camp, Mac's heart started beating faster. She could feel that they were onto something. She parked the Jeep, and the four of them piled out to meet the ground crew. Stan and his team remained in the air, searching for the old man.

The forensic team got to work after the area had been taped off. No one was to enter the area unless given permission and wearing protective equipment so as to preserve what could be evidence.

Mac and Burg took foot to survey the surrounding area to see if they could find anything. They walked northwest upstream toward their campsite a month earlier. Since they were there, the area had some rain and even one early snowstorm, so the creek bed was soggy and slippery. Due to this moisture, there were no footprints along the creek, so they decided that it was best to go back to the camp cave area and search for anything around there.

They did not want to disturb the forensic team as they were hard at work, but they could not just sit around on their hands either. They were both excited and nervous.

"You know, he could be nearby watching us," Burg whispered.

"I know. It has the hair on the back of my neck rising," Mac responded.

"If he is what I think he could be," Burg continued, "then we need to stay on high alert. This man is intelligent and highly dangerous, and we need to have each other's back."

Mac nodded in agreement. She felt like she was being hunted It was an odd gut feeling, but she tried to always follow her instincts. They usually did not lead her astray.

"I feel like we could be being hunted by him," Mac confirmed her thought bubble with words.

Burg reached for her hand. That was all that she needed. His reassurance.

Chapter 33

Mac often wondered why criminals killed law enforcement, and she had recently had this conversation with Burg. They both concurred on a few possibilities. One was to avoid arrest and prosecution for a crime already committed. Other people hold deep-seated hatred toward law enforcement due to past experiences, perceived injustices, or a general anti-authority sentiment.

Mental health plays a role in most crime and mental health issues; substance abuse or severe emotional disturbances can drive irrational behavior, including attacks on police officers.

Terrorism or ideological extremism can play a role as law enforcement symbolizes government or societal authority, making them a target for attack.

Organized crime or gang activity may play a role as in some gangs; status accompanies cop killing.

In other cases, personal conflicts or vendettas with specific officers can escalate to violence.

In the case of Deputy Dawg, it was a personal conflict or vendetta that pushed him to kill Sheriff Guy Howard Gaughnor in Nederland, Colorado. This gave Mac pause to think as to why someone would kill Sheriff Kane.

Kane was not a very nice guy, and he was not a great officer of the law, but he also wasn't in your face. He was just lazy and snarky and liked to make fun of other people at their expense. Most people do not care for this.

Mac wondered what really went down at the Last Chance Saloon. Did Kane smart off to the old man or vice-versa? Did they know each other? Had Kane arrested him in the past? Was it a personal thing?

Mac didn't know the answer, but she did know that Kane was dead, and this guy was on the lam, and it sure looked a lot like the facts she was garnering regarding Deputy Dawg in Nederland, Colorado.

Chapter 34

The area surrounding the cave was mountainous and steep and this inclimate early fall had brought moisture, making the ground cover slippery.

Mac and Burg were on foot surrounding the search area, Stan in the air and the forensics in the cave doing their work.

In the meantime, reporters were trying to find them.

Chapter 35

Kate Donnelly was known to be the best in the West in terms of reporting news in the region. She grew up wanting to be a sports reporter, and it was quite difficult for women to break into the news, let alone sports. They had to be picturesque in the form of a shapely woman weather girl to make it.

Kate did not want to report on snowstorms. She wanted to report on sports and manhunts. She wanted to break into the men's world of reporting and quite frankly she was without the genitalia to do it back in 1990 or even in the 2000's in the West.

She was a Wyoming gal, and it was so frustrating to her that the Suffrage Movement was met with less hostility than women reporting on sports and current events.

She was not going to let that stop her. There was a huge set of circumstances converging in the Bighorn Mountains with the possibility of Deputy Dawg or D. B. Cooper at the helm of a crime and she was not going to be stopped.

This was her moment.

Chapter 36

Sports reporting has been a male-dominated field since the beginning of time. Pioneering women have made strides.

The first trailblazer was Phyllis George who become one of the first female sportscasters when she joined CBS's "The NFL Today" in 1975.

Lesley Visser was another trailblazer, becoming the first woman to cover the NFL as a beat writer.

In the booth was tough. The camera could not focus on the physique of the reporter, so this barrier would prove to be a challenge.

Hannah Storm and Linda Cohn became prominent figures on ESPN, hosting and anchoring SportsCenter. Doris Burke made history as the first woman to be a full-time NBA game analyst.

Facing sexism, both on and off the air and behind the scenes, including harassment on social media, skepticism about their knowledge, experience, or expertise, and limited access would prove to be a giant barrier.

All of the above-mentioned women earned their gold in trying to break the glass ceiling for women in sports and reporting in general, and the queen of this hard-fought-for crown remains Kate Delaney.

Kate Delaney remains a prominent sports broadcaster and journalist and has built an empire over decades in syndicated sports talk shows and reporting on major radio networks.

Kate edged her way in by hosting The Kate Delaney Show which was a syndicated sports talk show, and this was her gateway to edge in the male-dominated sports world, and to edge out some male competitors who didn't do the homework she was willing to do in order to be crowned queen. Her hard work and dedication enabled her to be a regular contributor on major networks like NBC Sports Radio as it highlighted her knowledge of top competitors.

Kate did not achieve her goals without major hurdles. She attempted to gain access to sportscasting for years and ascertained hundreds of rejections. The glass ceiling was real, but for her, it was going to be fragile with cracks. The cracks were in the form of knowledge, tenacity, and work ethic. She was and remains a genius. She would outwork the competition and think outside of the box, and it has earned her the crown in which she shines.

Kate has interviewed U. S. Presidents, over 15,000 athletes, coaches, and sports personalities, including major players in the NBA, NFL, WMBA, and MLB. She has been honored at Super Bowls and can field "any grounder" bouncing her way.

She is also an advocate for women in many areas which made her a darling to most women familiar with her.

This was why Kate Donnelly was named in her honor.

Chapter 37

Mac was exhausted. She had not slept much in days or even weeks. This crime was growing in notoriety, and it put so much pressure on her.

She had the most excruciating year of her career between the Sheridan WYO Rodeo crimes and now this. It had been months of not much sleep.

In conjunction with the crimes that were not common to these parts, she had a new relationship with Burg. This caught her attention. She wanted this to work. He was of course not perfect but nor was she.

She wanted to get married to him, and this was a very new feeling. She did not fall in love with ease. She was peculiarly picky. She knew her worth. Men found her intimidating, and this annoyed her passionately. She was not really intimidating. She was sweet, kind, and genuine. She was also tenacious, talented, and hard-working. Insecure men found her intimidating, and for some odd reason, this was the unfortunate group of men in general who found her attractive.

Burg found her attractive but for the entirety of her being. It was not her outward beauty that was his only focus. She wasn't some Eastern European stunner. She was wholesome and athletic and wore a smile like a jewel.

It was also her intelligence, integrity, and grit that he was drawn to, and it was through their working relationship that they grew close. She would outwork him, and he was a workhorse. She would outwit him, and he was witty. She could outcharm anyone, and he was charming.

Most importantly to him, she loved him deeply and wholeheartedly without any sense of worry or reluctance. This was not something that Burg had ever experienced.

He held her hand as they scoured the area surrounding the cave. He could sense her reluctance to be there. Mac was no coward, but she had experienced trauma from men, and she was no fool. She was not about to let her guard down over a criminal, and she was tense. Her tension could be cut with a knife. The area was steep, and the boulders were large, surrounding this cave area.

It was challenging terrain. Burg had a modern walkie-talkie device to communicate with Stan and the ground crew, and Mac had a similar device with a solar charger attached to her backpack so that they could stay in contact with not only law enforcement but also the media. It was important to keep the media updated so that they didn't interfere with the investigation.

Mac chose Kate Donnelly as her main media contact because this young, tenacious reporter had integrity, intelligence, and true grit. Mac appreciated these characteristics highly.

Burg had his favorite as well. He communicated with his favorite media contact in Cheyenne. Leonard Crawford was known for his integrity intelligence, and experience in both reporting, but also, he was a man of nature and could speak to the terrain.

This was a dangerous area. It was steep and deep and there were coyotes and moose and bear and elk and deer. It was hibernation time for the bear, which meant that they needed to forage for food to hibernate and they were out and about in doing what nature needed them to do for survival.

This scenario added to the terrain and Leonard Crawford and Kate Donnelly were both adept at reporting in general, but they were also naturalists and could educate the nation on keeping an arms-length away from the investigation to preserve evidence first and foremost, but also to ensure that the investigation team was safe.

Mac and Burg were both concerned about the safety of the team and for themselves. This man was capable of anything, obviously, and Mac was intuitive about her personal safety. Burg was in love with her and was protective. He hovered over her while she negotiated the terrain. He had never wanted a woman like he wanted her. Her safety was his priority, even over catching a criminal.

Chapter 38

Burg heard it first. A hunter and a detective, he was savvy to movement. He put a hand on her chest in a communicative way, informing her that she needed to be on guard.

She stepped in close, and she watched him draw his weapon. Something was nearby. She did not know if it was a person or an animal, but either way, she was keenly aware that it was growing dark. Dusk was upon them, and they should have been back at the cave already. However, they had wandered out of range, and they were trying to find their way back.

It is easy to get lost in a forest, even if one is adept at mountaineering. All trees look the same at some point. The only differential can be the side the moss grows, the height of the tree, or any clearing boulder, or trail. They had wandered to a thick forest of no moss, no clearing, and no rocks. Just tall pines.

Burg was worried, and if Burg was worried, that meant trouble.

Chapter 39

Kate Donnelly was the first to go live that morning with the breaking news. She was always the early bird. Her grandmother used to remind her that the early bird got the worm, and she understood the metaphor.

It was not her first rodeo in reporting, but it was not going to be her last and she had met with Mac a day before she went with Burg to the mountains and had asked a personal favor.

"May I place a tag on you to track you for reporting purposes?" Kate asked.

Mac was confused. "A tag?"

Yes. There is a competitor of Apple, and I want to test it because it is a lot less expensive. I also want to be the first to know what happens in this investigation. I know this sounds invasive. It does not listen to you. It literally just tracks your location. It is supposed to be better than the competition because the satellite enhancer allows you to be what would otherwise be out of range, and it will still bounce off another satellite to continue tracking," Kate said.

Mac was aware that these devices were supposed to be accountable, but Mac had been hiking the Annapurna in Nepal a few years prior with her cousin, and their satellite phone did not work in the remote area of the Annapurna near Fishtail Peak.

Mac fell and she broke her kneecap, and their radio phone call for help did not work.

Mac had agreed to the tracker. What harm could it do? Kate was a reputable reporter, and she was hungry and enlightened about technology. It made sense to incorporate technology reporting and mountaineering. Therefore, Kate taped the device to Mac's left arm. It was as tiny as a button, and Mac had forgotten that it was there.

It would prove to save her life.

Chapter 40

D. B. Cooper was not Dan Cooper. Nor was he Deputy Dawg. They were one and the same, and Douglas Lewis's true identity was born.

Douglas Lewis was a chameleon. He could be a hippie. He could be a rocket scientist. He was a naturally gifted child born to two hippies who were nomadic and poor. He did not want to be poor. Nomadic was one thing. Poor was another.

He was a book learner, and he spent all of his nomadic poor childhood with books. There was always a public library around, and anyone could borrow a book. He studied history and engineering, mountaineering, and everything in between. He never had a formal education, and there were no birth records to identify him. He was never enrolled in school. He never saw a doctor. In the modern world of technology, he was a ghost.

He was intelligent, and he had squirreled the ransom money from the 1971 hijacking to the extent that he was able to live off the land for decades without a trace. He foraged for food and hunted wild game. He was undetectable and undetected in the Rocky Mountains of Wyoming. He was a wanted man in every state, but he was most wanted in Colorado for killing the sheriff in Nederland, and he was also most wanted in Oregon and Washington for hijacking an airplane.

His flight plan post-hijacking was Mexico City, and therefore, he figured that authorities would start the search for him on the West Coast and continue into Mexico and he was correct. That is exactly what they did.

Meanwhile, on foot, he made his way East over the Continental Divide on the Oregon Trail, and he made his way past Independence Rock in Wyoming near the Hole in the Wall where Butch Cassidy and the Sundance Kid hung out to try to evade law enforcement after being caught rustling cattle and robbing a bank.

Douglas Lewis lived off the land in all sorts of environments in Wyoming and ultimately settled in the Bighorn Mountains off the Red Grade, and had not seen much of civilization while living in a cave that used to be a bear's den until the old cow died. He took over her habitat after she passed, and he lived a reclusive existence until he went fishing one Fall afternoon, and a woman motioned for him to join her. She was attractive and welcoming, and she had a large trout on her line, so she landed with ease. He watched her from a distance at first. And when she detected his movement, he made his awareness known to her. She didn't flinch or recoil. In fact, the opposite. She motioned for him to use one of her worms, and he did.

He was then invited to join her for a fish fry, but he quickly disappeared. He'd already made a mistake. She had seen him.

Chapter 41

He could hear them whispering, and he wanted to hunt the hunted. He was not getting caught for this crime or any crime. He could outwit and outsmart them. He knew the land better than anyone else. He had lived in the area since 1972. He remained nomadic as he didn't want his whereabouts known.

He spotted Mac first. She was wearing jeans and a flannel shirt and had a small backpack on her back. She was holding hands with the man she was fishing with. He could not see the whole of the man, but just his right arm holding her left hand.

They were about to climb over a large boulder likely to get to higher ground and so he let go of her hand. He was in the midst of his climb when Lewis made his move. He was hiding behind a large pine tree and he darted toward her and grabbed her by the backpack. She let out a yelp as he put his right arm around her upper shoulders and neck.

"Burg!" she screamed. Burg turned around to see his fiancée captive to this old man.

The old man did not say a word, but he pulled her even tighter toward him. Burg didn't know what to do. He had no idea whether this man was armed, but her clearly owned a gun as he shot Sheriff Kane with a pistol.

Mac's eyes were wide as saucers, so she could not wiggle free. The more she tried, the tighter he gripped her. Burg saw the fear in her eyes, and he hated this man for it. He was reaching for his device to send an SOS to the ground crew and Stan, but the minute Lewis saw him reach for it, Lewis pulled the gun out of its holster with his left hand, and he placed it to her temple. She could feel the cold metal against her head, and her cortisone levels increased.

Burg took his hand off the device and put his hands in the air signaling that compliance would happen.

Lewis still had not said a word. Burg did not know what this man's demands were.

"What do you want from us," Burg asked.

Lewis did not respond. He just stood there with the gun aimed at Mac's head. Burg was unsure of what to do for one of the first times of his life. Seconds felt like decades. Burg wanted to rush them, but he was afraid that Lewis would make Mac, whether purposefully or accidentally.

Chapter 42

Kate Donnelly was monitoring the device that was attached to Mac's arm, and it showed that Mac had stopped moving. This concerned her as she had been watching Mac move since Kate assumed that she had met with the forensic team. Kate conferred with other reporters, and they concurred that something wasn't right Mac was nowhere near where the coordinates were conveyed to reporters that morning before Mac and his team headed up the mountain.

Kate and fellow reporters all went on camera to report their conjecture, and this alerted Stan's team in the air that something might be amiss. He radioed the forensic team, which had lost communications with Burg.

Stan took his copter up in the area and started circling lower and lower to the extent that it was safe to do so with wind sheer in the Bighorn Mountains. He could see where the forensic team was stationed as this was the coordinates shared, but he could not see any signs of Burg or Mac.

Kate reported her findings of Mac's coordinates based on the device that Kate had convinced Mac to wear on her arm. This was then communicated to Stan, who, in turn, plugged the coordinates into his helicopter computer. He headed in a northwesterly direction and slowed his speed and altitude to the extent that it was safe to do so.

Chapter 43

"What do you want from us," Burg pleaded with Lewis. "We can meet your demands if we know what they are."

Lewis had still not said a word. He finally spoke.

"I want to be left alone," Lewis said. He had no teeth and Mac almost threw up from his breath. He smelled like a dirty diaper.

"We can discuss you being left alone," Burg responded, knowing full well that this murderer was not going to be set free. "If you allow her to be free, we can begin discussions and negotiations," Burg said.

Lewis kept Mac in his grasp with the fun to her head.

It was a standoff.

Chapter 44

Stan spotted Burg up on a large boulder with his arms in the air. Then he saw Mac. She was standing near a tree with a man who had a gun to her head. Stan radioed it to all law enforcement in the state, and this made its way to the news. Stan's copilot pulled out his phone and took aerial video of this standoff, and he shared it with law enforcement, and one of the same quickly leaked it to the media. It went viral in no time.

When Kate Donnelly saw the footage, she quickly captured it and then went on the air first, explaining that it was her tag that gave Mac's coordinates, which led the aircrew to Mac, Burg, and the murderer. It was her clever idea that allowed Mac to be tracked.

Stan kept the circle tight on the helicopter and kept slowly lowering it to the point where Burg could feel the wave of the whirlybird. Burg was thrilled to see this man risking his life to help them.

This distraction gave the ground crew time to race to the coordinates where Mac was being held at gunpoint. The order given by the interim sheriff was to shoot to kill.

Chapter 45

The ground troops had them surrounded from a perimeter, and Stan held steady in his tight circle above. The sun was beginning to set and lighting would be an issue for Stan soon, but he was going to stay up for as long as he could.

Burg was slowly lowering his arms. The blood had flowed out of his fingers. He was trying to figure out how to get Mac away from Lewis without her being harmed.

All of a sudden, Burg heard a noise. It sounded like a branch snapping. It was his first clue that the perimeter was closing in. Within a minute, there were seven guns drawn on Lewis, and the interim sheriff was leading the charge. She had issued the order to take Lewis dead or alive, and she was hoping to fire the first shot.

"Drop your weapon," she commanded at Lewis. He did not drop the gun at Mac's temple. She shouted the command again but to no avail. He did not comply.

She took the first shot to his kneecap, and he buckled. Burg dashed off the boulder to grab Mac, and he almost tore his shoulder out of the socket with the force. He rolled her under him on the ground and crawled her to safety.

The ground force kept firing. It was suicide by a cop. It was a poetic ending to Douglas Lewis's life.

Chapter 46

Stan was able to safely land, and the entire crew met at the Last Chance Saloon in Bighorn, Wyoming, for a much-needed drink. The saloon was crowded with law enforcement and media, and folks were celebrating the capture of a career criminal and the safe return of law enforcement, especially Mac.

Mac and Burg were conducting interviews and answering questions about a whiskey and a steak, and Burg bought a round for the entire bar. He was so relieved that Mac was unharmed.

Mac felt like she was in an outer body experience and the existentialism of the moment would have to be recaptured at a later stage. She was exhausted and overwhelmed and grateful.

She was grateful for Burg, who stood by her, and for all law enforcement. She was especially grateful to Stan.

However, she owed a large part of this to a young, tenacious reporter who convinced her to wear a tag device, which might have ultimately saved her life. They all toasted Kate Donnelly. Her career would skyrocket, and she deserved it.

She had earned it the legitimate way.

Chapter 47

When the dust settled from the craziness of the past week, Mac had some time to reflect. She was back at work, and she was happy to be in her routine. The media had dissipated, and she could get in her early morning run without interference. She could snuggle with her rescue kittens, read a good book, and talk endlessly on the phone with Burg in the evenings.

He told her that he had an interview for the Sheridan Sheriff position the following Thursday and confirmed that he could stay with her for the weekend. He didn't need to ask. They had an open-door policy with staying with one another.

When Burg walked into the interview mid-morning that Thursday in November, they offered him the job right away. He was more than qualified, and it was a small town. The folks knew that he was engaged to their prosecuting attorney.

He buzzed to Mac's office to tell her about the news in person. She was thrilled. He would be giving his notice in Cheyenne and packing up, and his start date was December 1.

Chapter 48

It wasn't long before Burg was moved in and served as the Sheriff of Sheridan County. He was learning the ropes and learning about his new team, and it always took time to settle in.

Christmas was approaching, and Mac and Burg went up the Dayton-Cane side of the Bighorns to cut down their first Christmas tree together. They brought it home on the top of her Jeep and set it up in their living room.

They were settling in to watch National Lampoon's Christmas and listening to the kittens run amok in the Christmas tree when Mac grew serious. Burg had just built a fire, and they were about to snuggle under a blanket on the couch.

He noticed a shift in her demeanor.

"What going on in the pretty little head of yours," he asked.

She didn't answer for a minute.

"I want to get married this weekend," she said.

Burg was surprised. They had talked about getting married the next summer in the mountains. They had talked about a quiet small gathering.

"I want to throw a huge Christmas party here and I want to get married here in our home with lots of friends around. I know that Judge Redle would marry us here. She lives only a few blocks away."

Burg was shocked but pleased. He did not want to wait until summer.

"Then that's what we will do."

Chapter 49

The wedding was stunning. The house was festive with holiday decorations and the music was lively. Mac walked down the staircase in her rose-colored gown with feather lines three-quarters length sleeves with a gorgeous long veil decorated with beads of florals.

Burg was in a formal tux. He had never worn one before, and he could not believe how uncomfortable the shoes were.

Nevertheless, they had about 75 friends and family in the house three days before Christmas and Judge Redle officiated in her judicial robe.

They feasted and drank and danced late into the evening and it was a night of perfection.

Chapter 50

Life settled in for Mac and Burg. They still had a reasonably large fallout from the Donald Lewis case. There were conspiracy theorists who did not believe that it was D. B. Cooper who committed the crime. No one questioned the Deputy Dawg portion.

Nevertheless, Mac continued in her role as County Prosecutor and Burg was setting in as the Sheridan County Sheriff.

The shining star of the incident was Kate Donnelly. She was offered a position at CBS in New York City as an investigative reporter, and she accepted it with grace and gratitude and the hunger of a young journalist.

Mac was proud of Kate. She was named after the all-time GOAT. Kate Delaney.

www.ingramcontent.com/pod-product-compliance
Lightning Source LLC
LaVergne TN
LVHW040034120125
800981LV00001B/126